REACH FOR JOY

A MEMOIR

TESSY L REYS

Inquiries about additional permissions should be

directed to: northwestsourdough@gmail.com

Editor – Kathryn Galan

Cover designer – Scott Deyett

Proofreader – Verushka Byrow

Published by Northwest Sourdough

Print ISBN 978-0-9854-6145-4

Library of Congress Control Number: 2015914624

DEDICATION

I would like to dedicate this story to all ten of my children and to victims of abuse everywhere who are still suffering in silence.

With deep gratitude I would like to thank all of those who supported me and helped me put the pieces back together after I escaped thirty years of abuse. You know who you are.

Also, I offer thanksgiving to my beloved parents, and finally, to the one who whispered, "You have the key in your own hand, and you always have."

I felt as if society, religion, and life had conspired against me, imprisoning me in a hopeless marriage without any means of escape. But it was I who lived unaware, with my head in the sand. There was no one I could blame except the woman in the mirror.

— *TLR*

CONTENTS

AUTHOR'S NOTE

If you are reading this story hoping to find a monster who chains victims to the wall and beats them, you are reading the wrong story. Abusers are often portrayed as complete villains, but the truth is often quite complicated. Like everyone else, a controlling person can also have a nice side. In fact, some narcissists are masters at carefully meting out kindness: just enough crumbs to keep their victim off balance and under their control. Life as a victim is anything but predictable and is often a darkening spiral as the abuser takes control little by little, crippling the victim's self-esteem and erasing their boundaries. It can be near impossible to escape from the clutches of a narcissist. My hope is that other victims might find help or gain courage from my story—and so change their own story.

PREFACE

*When a mother is happy her baby has died, there is
something terribly wrong.*

I STROKED HIS SMALL BODY LOVINGLY, BUT HE DIDN'T MOVE. As I gazed
down at this newborn son of mine, with his head missing above the
brow, the hollow space inside me grew. The stethoscope was like a
circling vulture, waiting for his heart to stop.

"He's gone," the doctor whispered quietly.

My arms cradled him, these arms that had held so many babies.
Babies, babies... I'd had babies in my arms since I *was* a baby. He had
a face but no crown to his head, no brain. I'd had to push him out
with such force that his little face was squished, because he had no
skull to protect it.

They laid him in a crib near my hospital bed. In the night, I got
up to go to the bathroom and passed by him. As I glanced down, I
was gruesomely shocked. Hours after his death, his face had become
shriveled and purple, the sharp edge of his brow sloping back to
nothingness. He was swaddled in soft blankets. The small cap that
attempted to cover his missing skull had fallen away and exposed
dark tissue. I was traumatized.

"Cry for your baby," the nurse said gently. "You must cry."

"I can't." My eyes were void of healing tears. I was raw like a raked flesh wound. Yet, I was happy, and my heart, exulted. The internal division caused by simultaneous sorrow and exultation was a terrible anguish to bear; it was like being split in two.

"My baby, my sweet angel, you died in my arms as I stroked your body with caresses. I saw you in my mind's eye, above my hospital bed, as your soul fled your damaged body. You waved goodbye to me and said you loved me. I love you, sweetie. Go where you can't suffer or be hurt like your brothers and sisters."

When a mother is happy her baby has died, there is something *terribly* wrong. I was too far gone to realize that then, but I know it now.

You might think it strange for a bunch of young men to be scattered across someone's backyard, sleeping off their adventures. But these were my oldest brother's friends who had returned in the wee hours of the morning from their bachelor romp at Yosemite, and, having nowhere else to sleep, they'd flopped down in my parents' backyard. This was considered perfectly normal at the time.

If I had known then what was to come, I would have altered my steps and never visited the backyard on that cold spring morning. The California sun, which had started its trek across the clear sky, was totally oblivious to what had just happened, but that moment altered my life forever.

*   *   *

Jason didn't pursue me, but he came around, hung out with my family, the Reys, and began playing his banjo with my brother's bluegrass band. I guess that gave him a reason to loiter, since the band often practiced at our house. My oldest brother, Bruce, had a bedroom separate from the main house, accessed from an outside door, which was good, because his friends could go in and out to pee in the bushes without bothering anyone.

I had recently found out that Jason's older brother, Keith Gannon, was upset with me because I'd never written to him back when he was in the army. Apparently, he'd sent me some letters, which I never received because Bruce had intercepted them. I was surprised because, except for one boy in high school whom I had declined to marry, I hadn't really dated at all and had never imagined that anyone could be interested in me.

The same week after meeting Jason, Keith came over and sat down on the porch stairs next to me. I let him know I was sorry for never replying to his letters but I don't think he believed me. I felt bad, so I tried to give him a little Cracker Jack toy as a consolation gift—a good example of how immature I was at the time. Then, one of my little brothers came up and grabbed it, demanding,

"That's mine. Give it to me." I felt embarrassed. Maybe it *had* been my brother's toy, who knows? In large families… there aren't many boundaries.

Although it had been humiliating, I wasn't attracted to Keith. I was attracted to his younger brother, Jason, the guy I had found in my backyard. It only took me a week to fall hard for him. He was emotionally detached, obviously smart, and pretty good on the banjo.

I started to hang around my brother and his friends—with any excuse I could—just to be near Jason. On their next trip to Yosemite, Bruce invited me to go along. That was cool, because my big brother had recently returned from the service, hadn't started his life yet, and had never liked me hanging around before. While he was enlisted, he had come home once, super handsome in his military uniform, and had given me a hug. Previous to that, he had been distant and exclusive, like big brothers can be.

There had been one other time, before he joined the service when he took me for a drive in his car and offered me his funny cigarette. It was like a little sausage rolled up, and the smoke wafting over his head smelled sweet, like burning herbs or leaves. I took a few puffs and the world slowed down. I felt like a fish slipping through a liquid paint stream, sort of like being warm, wonderful, and alive while you are asleep. I never smoked that again—it was too weird for me, especially since it felt strange not having my bearings.

So, I went to Yosemite and tagged after Jason. He mentioned that I needed to lose weight.

"Women usually get fat later in life… May as well not start out that way," he stated, while shooting tobacco juice from his lips. Jason preferred rail-thin women. He talked about what women should be like and how they should wear dresses and grow their hair long. He added, "Women should stay home and mind the house, sew, and cook."

I didn't like sewing and hated dresses, but I was a pretty good cook.

I was like a puppy tagging around after him and was willing to do whatever he wanted.

At one point while we were walking along the trails, he told me about Celine, a girl he'd met at the Yosemite square dance on his last trip. Then he suddenly glanced over his shoulder. *"Run,"* he yelled and sped off, leaving me bewildered.

My brother and his other friends had been following behind us when they all took off running, as well. Being clueless, I just stood there... and got attacked by a swarm of yellow jackets... *Then* I ran! It turned out that my brother Bruce had spied a yellow jacket nest and launched a rock at it. Everyone else knew that if someone ran, you had better run, too. Everyone else except me. And that's how I got stung all over by yellow jackets.

Throwing a rock at a wasp's nest wasn't a surprising act for my brother. Bruce had a long history of being a goof-off and getting into petty trouble. With his gap-tooth grin and dark wavy hair, he often wore cutoffs and a sheepskin leather vest and looked very much like Jesus. He and Keith Gannon had been best friends most of their lives. They were often into some kind of mischief and were frequent flyers when it came to getting their knuckles rapped by the black-frocked nuns in our parochial school. Bruce was irreverent and crude, but he couldn't repress his generous, loving heart, even if he'd wanted to.

He would be pissed off if he knew I told you this, but he still plays Secret Santa year 'round; he started when he was just a young boy delivering papers. With his first paycheck, he went out and bought all of his many siblings a lollipop. I still remember that big red sucker molded like a raspberry with bumps on one side.

FALLING IN LOVE

He instructed me to plait one small braid on the side of my hair and wear flowers in it, so I did that, too. I was no longer recognizable to my family and friends as the person I once was.

As cold spring mornings turned into warm summer days, Jason and I spent more time together. Or maybe I should say Jason seemed to be more tolerant of me hanging around. He was aloof, didn't talk much, and incessantly played his banjo, which had been fashioned with his own hands. He was very talented and could handcraft anything. The neck of the instrument had an inlaid mother-of-pearl design and hand-carved scrollwork. It was a beautiful, worn banjo that had obviously seen the back bed of a truck too often.

I fell hard. How filled with love and desire I was for him! When he wasn't around, it felt like a piece of me was missing. I longed to have him pursue me and was willing to do anything for him. I whipped up a batch of maple fudge and baked him a chocolate walnut cake. *Ha!* He didn't like sweets! I cleaned up the spilt spit-toon mess after the men got into playing their music and someone's boot kicked it over. That sure impressed his friends. (My poor dad once accidentally picked up a bottle of beer to take a sip, thinking it was his, but it was filled with spittoon juice! *Gag!* It was a disgusting habit, and all of the Dirty Cowboys indulged in it.)

On one warm night, the sand flew under my feet as I chased behind Jason and we hid in the sand dunes. We were all playing hide and seek on the beach under the lingering summer twilight. Earlier, Jason had hoisted me into his jacked-up camo-painted '64 Chevy truck, and we'd taken off for the beach to hang out with the other unkempt cowboys. He no longer talked about Celine, the Yosemite girl.

As summer deepened and the parched brown hills shimmered in a haze, I began to wear long prairie skirts and dresses exclusively. I scavenged these out-of-date clothes from thrift stores and wore them to please and impress Jason. His mother wore long dresses too, and a head covering; people often mistook her for a nun. The whole neighborhood considered Mrs. Gannon odd, but she was the one they went to when they needed help. She told me that any decent woman wore a dress. "No need for women to dress like men," she said.

Jason encouraged me to wear floor-length dresses, but he also liked me to wear short shorts and skimpy summer dresses when his mamma wasn't around. He instructed me to plait one small braid on the side of my head and wear flowers in my hair, so I did that, too. My family and friends no longer recognized me as the person I had once been.

Before I knew it, I was immersed in Jason's fantasy world of life from two hundred years ago. He wanted to live off the grid and have nothing to do with society. By fall, we were sneaking off to be alone. We spent time under the stars up in the hills, with coyotes yapping nearby and the intox-icating late-summer smell of sunbaked weeds in the surrounding fields. My heart beat wildly as I lay next to him in my sleeping bag under the rising moon. I yearned to be with him in his thick, rolled-up wool blanket that his mom had crocheted. He spoke to me in the darkness and told me stories of the white ghost woman who roamed those very hills—near Lamar, where Jason's family lived—and the street fights he had been in when he was younger. Nearby, he had his Colt .45 special and holster belt lined with hand-poured lead bullets. I felt safe. I couldn't imagine life without him; he filled my world.

I was amazed that there was so much more to life than minding kids, dirty diapers, and washing dishes. Jason showed me many new things: how to crosscut large logs with a jerry-rigged chainsaw; how to cook beans right in the can over an open fire; the best way to bake an apple pie (it had to be done his way, with the apples diced into small even pieces); and even how to machine small tools needed for projects. He had a shop in his parents' garage, a smelter for melting metal (the whole volunteer fire department showed up one day in response to the billowing smoke), and made his own large-caliber shotgun casings from a mold he had fashioned himself. I soaked up the attention, something I'd never had much of.

Once I witnessed a can of beans blow up on the campfire and spray a fine mist over those present. It was a hint that he did not know *everything*. When the can of beans exploded, I automatically, without thinking, flew into another man's arms to protect me—and not Jason's.

That summer, we spent time target shooting. I blew cans off of a fence or shot a bell hanging in the field. I did not have the strength to shoot his Colt .45. He probably regretted showing me how to shoot a gun, though; I outshot him every time during target practice. By that point, we were spending all of our time together. The flush of new love made me giddy. I had never been so intoxicated before.

Jason considered himself to be too smart for school, so he had dropped out of ninth grade and began living in the hills above his hometown. He was determined to live life like the mountain men did centuries earlier. I was fascinated and challenged by his aloof manner, his many talents, and his intelligence. He obviously enjoyed my admiration. I don't think he was aware that he was a con artist or a controlling man; he was just always right, and other people were stupid (in Jason's estimation). Although scoring the highest IQ in my class, I was a perfect candidate for the "stupid list," easy to manipulate—and brainwash.

The Dirty Cowboys worked on building a hand-hewed cabin up in the foothills where Jason hung out. I was soon helping out on the ever-unfinished cabin—anything to spend time with him.

There were plenty of things to do. As the fireplace took shape, I mixed mortar, selected, carried, and helped cut the stones. Jason showed me how to run plumb lines, use a plumb bob, a square and also how to use a tube you filled with water to find the level.

I also loved baking bread in a ground oven he fashioned for me. He dug the hole early in the morning and then built a fire in it. The soil was adobe, so it absorbed the heat and turned into brick at the same time. When he felt it was hot enough, he scooped out the ashes, and I placed a loaf pan of bread dough into the ground and covered the hole. The bread turned out a little burnt around the edges, but it was delicious! I learned many other "mountain man" things, like how to cut all of the fat off venison before cooking it to moderate the wild gamey flavor; how to pour molten lead into bullet molds; how to scrape a hide; and even how to stitch up rawhide moccasins. Eventually, I took over more of the camp cooking and baking, which was only right, "since I was a woman."

*   *   *

Being in the outdoors, learning new skills, and doing something besides changing diapers opened the door to a whole new world for me. I inhaled the scent of mountain sagebrush and enjoyed crunching through the oak leaves that littered the slopes. The woody, smoky smell of venison sizzling over campfires in blackened camp skillets tantalized me. Ground squirrels popped their little noses out of burrows; unknown creatures rustled in the underbrush; and ranch cows lowed on the distant Lamar hills. It was a magical, mesmerizing time in my life.

We were camped out in the foothills early one morning when I witnessed Jason shoot at (and miss) a very large retreating mountain lion. In the distance was the old bell we used for target practice, nailed to its post, just beyond the place where the majestic creature made its escape.

On another occasion, I watched as Jason dressed out a fresh road-kill deer and hung it from a tree. He showed me where the glands on the legs of the buck were and then explained how to avoid damaging them, so as not to ruin the meat's flavor.

After struggling to start the camp fire unsuccessfully, I perched on
a log in a long prairie dress and watched as he gave me instructions.

"Most people can't start a fire," he explained. "You need to build
a support with the wood to allow oxygen into the fire, not just pile
the wood on top of itself."

Little did I know how handy that knowledge would be in the future.

*   *   *

In my own way, I thought I was pretty. I had brownish-blonde hair
(more commonly known as dirty, dishwater blonde). I'd inherited
my dad's hazel eyes and my mother's perfect complexion.

"I like my women thin," Jason nonchalantly remarked to me one
morning—again—and then continued, "If you lose weight, I will
marry you."

If I would change for him and become what he wanted, he would marry me...

If a red flag had hit me between the eyes, I probably wouldn't
have noticed. Actually, I didn't even *know* about red flags. Instead, I
was thrilled—but it probably scared Jason a bit—when the weight
melted off me so quickly. I had fallen for him and not only believed
everything he said, but was willing to do whatever he wanted. It
was a way to escape my narrow life, though I didn't realize it then.
I just thought I was in love. Jason became the authority, and my
parents suddenly became ignorant.

In high school health class, we learned how you might get bacteria that could potentially eat away your face and brain if you had
sex with an infected person, or how going barefoot in the South
was risky because of the worms that could crawl through the soles
of your feet and live inside you. But the things I really needed to
learn about were red flags, boundaries, and toxic relationships.
Unfortunately, no one taught courses on those subjects—oh yeah—
or how to sign a check, change the oil in a car, or grill a steak—skills
you might really need in life.

* * *

Although I had taken driver's training in high school and had practiced on the back roads at my aunt's farm as a young teenager, I still
didn't have my license that summer. But I did have wanderlust and
wanted to travel. When I turned eighteen, I worked up my courage
and finally felt ready to get my license, so I asked my dad to help
me. You know how it is—you put yourself out there, stretch a little
further than you are comfortable with, realizing in your heart that
everything rides on the outcome and then... *boom!*... you get shot
down. Sometimes—way down.

It was a turning point in my life when my dad declined to help me
get my license. In retrospect, I could have asked someone else to help
me, but my self-confidence and self-esteem were shot. I wondered,
Was there something wrong with me? I didn't know then but later learned
that he refused to help all of my other siblings get their licenses as
well. He was afraid to teach *any* new driver; it wasn't just me.

His words rang in my heart for decades: "You can't drive. You
are too immature and not ready."

It's strange how a moment can change your life. The stage was
set for what was to come. Because I believed him, I ended up being
able to find work only within walking distance and had to find rides
to get to my college art classes. I continued to live with my parents
because without my driver's license, I didn't have many options.

When I talked to Jason about teaching me to drive (I was twenty),
he said, "Women should stay at home and not gallivant."

I wasn't sure about that.

"A man should always know where his woman is. I will take you
wherever you want to go," he lied. I was too naive to realize he was a
compulsive liar and would say whatever was necessary to be in control.

I was uncertain, but when you are in love for the first time, you
believe almost anything. I had so little experience with men that I
trusted him. Instead of facing my fear, I gave into it. In doing so, I
gave away a piece of myself. My self-esteem and self-confidence
took another blow.

Slowly, one by one, my weak boundaries were erased, either by encouragement, disapproval, or pressure. If there was something I didn't want to do or choices I wanted to make that Jason didn't like, he would sulk, lie, disappear, ridicule, and then use persuasion, force, or silent disapproval to change my mind.

He didn't like my family and objected to me hugging or kissing my parents; he showed his disapproval by sulking, leaving or saying privately to me that it was wrong to kiss and hug other people. Jason told me how ugly I looked in pants and that women shouldn't wear them. He also despised short hair on women and felt women were ruining the world; that they were bad drivers and the cause of car wrecks; and that they shouldn't vote because they voted wrong, so a man should have his wife's vote.

I wanted to believe him. If I didn't agree with him, I knew he would leave and not come back, and I didn't feel I could face that. Being immature and gullible, I was eager to turn myself into whatever he wanted. How could I have known that this would eventually make me miserable? I just wanted his approval and love. He did not know how to love, and only bestowed approval when he got his way. Like so many people with low self-esteem and poor boundaries, I was eager to become whatever *someone else* wanted, instead of being myself and finding someone who liked me the way I was.

*   *   *

Jason bought me a treadle sewing machine from the local weekend flea market for forty dollars. It was a hybrid machine that had a treadle and an electric motor.

After all, "Every woman should know how to sew," was his reasoning.

In previous efforts to sew with my mother's old Ward machine, I had been so desperately frustrated that, during one impossible session, I had thrown the machine in the garbage, "where it belongs." My family still jokes about that incident. I had an impatient, impulsive nature. So I wasn't thrilled about the sewing machine at first.

However, since it was my very own machine, I began to sew simple aprons and quilt blocks. Before long, I graduated to floor-length, flounced prairie dresses and—I cringe to say it now—even bonnets! Next was a double-breasted western shirt for Jason, complete with antler buttons that he fashioned by hand. I loved to take on a challenge and conquer it. I guess obtaining Jason's love was a challenge for me, and I wanted to conquer him.

With some reservations, both families thought we were a good fit; more likely, our parents were relieved to have us, already in our twenties, get on with our lives. I didn't listen to what my head said, only my heart. *Didn't everyone have a good and a bad side? Things would turn out well if we loved each other, right?*

It takes two to be in a mature, loving relationship—too bad I didn't realize that sooner. I couldn't figure out what to do about babies, either. I was Catholic and so was he. Birth control was taboo for Catholics, and I had been determined not to get married or have children. At least I had once felt that way.

I gave my virginity to him in the cornfield one autumn night. The moon was full and the night hushed by Indian summer warmth. Passionate expectation filled my heart, but Jason turned out to be a selfish lover and I was disappointed. The line, however, had been crossed and there was no going back. (Read this as: once a man hits a homerun, he is unwilling to go back to first base.) As a passionate, affectionate person, I poured my heart into my love… but it was one-sided.

CHAPTER 2:
DECADE 1, YEAR 1980

YOU MARRIED ME, NOW YOU BELONG TO ME

Before the wedding, Jason confronted the priest and demanded that we use the wedding vows in which the woman promises to obey her husband. The priest answered that, in the Catholic tradition, the man and woman vow to honor and respect one another. I listened to their exchange and a seed of fear sprouted.

JASON NEVER ACTUALLY ASKED ME TO MARRY HIM. There was no engagement. Instead, we talked about getting married and then went to the courthouse and got the license. We took the blood tests, and, about that time, I found out I was pregnant.

Our families squabbled over the best time to have the wedding, so we ended up getting married the last weekend before the marriage license was set to expire. Jason fashioned a wedding ring from a copper and bronze pipe fitting. He did not want to wear a ring, so I made him a brown and white western-style shirt for the wedding. I bought a cream-colored chiffon dress from Sears for fifty dollars. My one bridesmaid was my older sister, Lynn. She wore the long blue dress I had sewn for a trip to Yosemite.

Our families and friends put together a potluck barbeque reception in my parents' backyard, the same backyard where I had found Jason that long-ago morning with his coat wrapped around his neck. Jason's sister made the wedding cake. His best man forgot the ring and delayed the ceremony. Then, with our first child already in my womb, I walked down the aisle on my father's arm, the first of his twelve children to wed. I was apprehensive. Secretly, I'd hoped for a romantic engagement and looked forward to a bridal shower, but Jason was not one for romance—he ignored our first Valentine's Day, much to my dismay—and no one remembered to give me a bridal shower. These kinds of events confirmed an inner suspicion that something was wrong with me and that I somehow deserved to be forgotten.

Before the wedding, Jason confronted the priest and demanded that we use the wedding vows in which the woman promises to obey her husband. The priest answered that, in the Catholic tradition, the man and woman vow to honor and respect *one another*. As I listened to their exchange, a seed of fear sprouted. Briefly, I wondered about a divorce, if things went bad. But being a dutiful Catholic, I brushed the thought away. Besides, I was with child and could envision no other path. Even though I had been one of the top two students in my parochial school class, I *obviously* (sarcasm intended) was too stupid to drive, which made getting an education or a decent job out of reach. My choices seemed to be either to get married or stay stuck at home for my whole life. It was the kind of desperate black-and-white thinking that a teenager would have.

I knew my parents would be disappointed but loving about my condition. But Jason was horribly embarrassed and strongly warned me not to tell anyone. His parents would be devastated by the news of my pregnancy, since sex and love were taboo subjects in the Gannon household. So we pretended that the baby came early, as if that fooled anyone. That was the beginning of many lies. I had a transparent, open heart, and lying did not come natural to me. Jason, on the other hand, could twist anything until it became truth to him. He was adamant that I do so as well.

Married Life

At first, we lived in my bedroom in my parents' house, until Jason found a small eight-foot trailer that was covered in filth inside and out. He parked the derelict in the orchard and couldn't wait to show me his "good deal." It had been used to store medications in a cattle field for ranch animals. Apparently, the door had been left open too long because the trailer was filled with dirt, mold, bird droppings and rodent excrement. We cleaned it out, and it became our first home together.

It foreshadowed what was to come.

Jason was employed as a finish carpenter during the winter months, and then when the slow season came along, he would gal-livant. He built some of the finest mansions, in the midst of avocado orchards, on the Central California coast, from the slab all the way up to the finish carpentry. I went to work with him and learned to hang doors, lay out a foundation, pour a slab so the cream would come to the top and make a hard surface, wire a building, tape and mud drywall, and even how to pound a nail correctly so it wouldn't split the wood. I also sanded, wielded the shovel, and did the cleanup.

Sometimes, while working, we would plan the layout and design of our dream house that we were going to build together.

We imagined open-lofted ceilings and unique bathtubs made with our own hand-crafted tiles. Being artistic, I had a lot to offer when it came to design and beauty. Having a beautiful home became my life dream, and I was filled with hope for the future. Although he lacked a formal education, Jason was very skilled with his hands. He made twice the going wage for a finish carpenter and was in high demand for the quality of his workmanship. How proud I was of my handsome, talented husband.

*   *   *

We moved into the tiny trailer, under the skimpy shade of the apricot trees. One early morning soon after, I lay in bed, my stomach churning with morning sickness.

Jason nudged me. "Get up and make my breakfast."

"I'm feeling sick," I groaned.

Then, with his next words, he destroyed our newly fledged marriage.

"I did not get married to have to get up and make my own breakfast." There was a hard edge to his voice.

So, trying to ignore the rising gorge, I got up and made his breakfast. I felt diminished and ashamed. I had assumed he would care about my condition and react in a loving manner. I was wrong.

If somehow, I could have known what lay ahead, maybe I would have had the courage, at that moment, to walk out, slam the door as hard as I could, and bring our baby up alone. His tone had been harsh; there was nothing loving about it. He was making sure we got off to the right start—and that I *obeyed* him.

He now owned me; I was his wife. I belonged to him, and would do as I was told.

Decades later, he would tell his sons that it was a man's Christian duty to make sure his wife was obedient. But in that moment, only a short time after the honeymoon, I realized that I had made a terrible mistake.

The honeymoon was over.

Overcome with fear and embarrassment, I found that I did not have the courage to stand up for myself. Because I allowed him to treat me that way, from that moment forward, Jason owned me. I was an object—his possession. I was afraid of him and ashamed to admit it. Gone was the love and joy I had hoped for in my marriage. Once I realized that he didn't love me, fear became my taskmaster.

A Series of Hovels

The first place we lived, after various trailers, was an old warehouse over a dry creek bed. It was overrun by little furry creatures whose calling cards were black pellets and a yellow, potent-smelling residue.

At that point, we had been married almost two years and had previously taken up residence in my bedroom—after the honeymoon, in the eight-foot trailer that Jason found in a field; and then in a nicer trailer that had been owned by Jason's younger brother, Joshua. We were living in Joshua's trailer when our first son, Ryan, was born, but then Joshua sold the trailer, so we had to move.

We then graduated to the warehouse, which I dubbed "The Mouse House." Soon after we moved in, during one of Jason's off-seasons from building and finish carpentry, I found myself pregnant with our second child; my first born was nine months old. The only food in the house at that moment was a bag of pancake mix and a box of potatoes. Being from a huge Catholic family, I had been brought up not to expect luxuries, but my parents had always made sure we had enough to eat and a decent home.

"Well, pancakes it is," I sighed. As I scooped some mix into a bowl, I noticed mouse pellets sprinkled throughout. *Ugh!* Fried potatoes had been getting tiresome at that point. I was pregnant, still nursing my first baby, and hungry. Grabbing a strainer out of a drawer— which also had a scattering of mouse raisins—I strained the mix, added water, and that night we dined on mouse-urine pancakes.

Jason didn't seem to care that there wasn't any food in the house. He had a nonchalant, "mountain-men-don't-give-a-fig" attitude. While living as a bachelor in the cabin on the foothills above Lamar, he had lived off a pot of unrefrigerated, homemade beans for a week at a time. He also made his own liquor, hunted for deer, and, when food was really scarce, he tried eating bugs. So mouse pancakes didn't faze him. And if *he* could eat it, he figured, everyone else could eat it, too.

"Hard times are good for the character," he was fond of saying.

* * *

Rent was cheap for the cavernous warehouse, but we only took up part of it. A man who worked on appliances rented out the remainder of the space. It was a cold, rough, unfinished place. I tried to keep the piecemeal carpets clean, especially when Ryan started to crawl around on the floor, but it was impossible, so I had to keep him in a playpen. Mouse feces were heavily scattered throughout the building—it was no place for a baby or any human, for that matter. Jason set mouse traps, but, after catching twenty-one in a short period of time and disposing of so many broken-necked creatures, he felt it was a useless task.

In the dark at night, while in bed, I could hear the gnawing, squeaks, and skittering, as the rulers claimed their territory. The pockets of our clothing that hung in the closet were filled with poop and matted nests made from chewed-up clothes. I cleaned out the rank kitchen drawers constantly, but it was futile. We fell asleep to the symphony each night and awakened to it, too, when it grew too loud to ignore.

My kitchen floor was dark reddish brown. It had a fine grooved design and didn't show dirt, so I could be lazy and not mop it every day. That made up for having to clean poop out of the drawers and cabinets on a daily basis. I bathed my baby Ryan in the sink; he loved to splash the soapy water everywhere. Sometimes, when the weather was nice, I put him in a large mixing bowl full of warm water, set it outside on the back porch, and let him splash all he wanted. I was uncomfortably pregnant, and it was nice to spend time outside, watching my baby play as the freshly-washed diapers flapped their wings on the line strung out beyond the porch.

* * *

The micro-ants crawled up my hand so quickly that I threw the piece of banana bread across the room. Blind without my glasses on and still lying in bed, I hadn't noticed that the miniature army had taken over my morsel on the bedside table. As I reached into the little zip bag to claim my bite of bread, I felt a swarm crawl all over my hand and up my arm. I was hoping to keep the morning sickness at bay by having an early-rising snack, but between the mice and the ants, I soon realized that I would have to come up with another idea. At that point, the best idea seemed to be getting out of bed to eat.

I cracked open some farm-fresh eggs that were given to me by a neighbor who had her own chickens. The first couple of eggs were frying up in the skillet when I noticed that they looked a bit funny— somewhat thick, chunky, and just weird. Jason wouldn't care, so I fed him the eggs with some bacon, and he was fine with it. Then I cracked another egg for my breakfast—oh yuck, *barf, ewww*! There was a dead, partially-formed baby chick inside. Of course, with morbid curiosity, I had to check out the rest of the eggs.

I took them outside and cracked them open. They *all* contained either dead baby chicks or were rotten smelling, with funny-looking egg yolks like the ones I'd fed Jason. I had no idea how long the eggs had been sitting outside in the woman's yard. My guess was she didn't know, either. Jason was lucky he didn't die. I could imagine the newspaper headline: *Wife Kills Husband with Rotten Eggs.*

It wasn't the only morning my breakfast surprised me.

Frying up bacon was pretty standard—throw it in the pan, cook lots (when we had it) because Jason liked to eat lots, then pour the hot bacon grease into an old coffee can perched on the back of the oven so that I could either dispose of it later or give it to my sister-in-law for her dogs. She said that it made the dogs' coats shiny and soft.

Not a problem, right? One morning, as I poured the sizzling-hot grease into the coffee can, a high, piercing *squeak* suddenly filled the air. With horror, I witnessed a mouse jump up and down in the simmering grease, screaming in agony as it died. *That* explained my brother-in-law's earlier cryptic comment about dead mice in the bacon grease. I assured him I would never dispose of mice in the bacon grease and then give it to them for their dogs. Unbeknownst to me, I had done just that. I could just see the next headline: *Woman Drowns Mice in Boiling Grease and Tries to Poison Dogs with It!*

* * *

A crocheted christening dress for the baby stirring in my womb grew, stitch by stitch, from my busy hands. I also taught myself how to knit. It wasn't enough for me to learn to knit a potholder. My first project had to be a pair of baby leggings with ribbing at the top and ankles. Plus, it needed a gusset in the crotch. I had to use four needles to shape the legs and feet and circular needles around the waist and hips. I always seemed to dive in, hoping for the best.

I no longer enjoyed my art. Jason tried to tell me what to draw and how to draw it. He wanted to control my art and commercialize it by having me paint cutesy angel plaques to sell. Of course, *he knew best.* We got into an argument when he insisted the artwork I had done in college, some of which were nudes done in my Life Drawing class, had to be destroyed.

"These drawings are no better than porn. Your parents never should have allowed you to take a class with nude models in it. They should be destroyed. You've committed a mortal sin, and I won't have these pictures in my house." Jason grabbed the drawings and walked out of the room. I was mortified and a flush of shame spread through my body. I knew there was nothing to be ashamed of, but his anger scared me, so I let him destroy my drawings. With their destruction, a piece of me withered.

After that, with the exception of a few false starts, I gave up art. It was something sacred that I felt he had no right to interfere with. I was taught that the human body was beautiful and that love and sex were gifts from God, who is a loving father. My art was beautiful—at least *I* thought so, and so did my parents. My high school art instructor told me I was the most talented artist that he had seen in his many years as a teacher. My art had defined me since I was two years old.

I couldn't allow him to control my art, so I gave it up.

* * *

Ryan, our firstborn, had arrived in the spring of 1981. Having a baby gave me purpose. I had no idea that one's own baby could pull so

powerfully on the heart. Jason told me early on that once children
came, I could give my affection
to them, as he didn't want it.
So I poured affection and love
into my children and withdrew
it from him. How proud I was
that my son grew fast and was
so smart. I didn't have long to
wait before the next baby
arrived.

The pains came on in the night, accompanied by the choir of mice.
It was early, maybe 3:00 a.m. After a while, I got up and made my
way to the kitchen. I proceeded to make up some cherry tarts for
Jason, as I knew he would need something to eat when he got up. I
figured a treat would be nice, and I needed to do something while I
labored. Later that day, I delivered a beautiful baby girl, and Jason
named her Aleena. I was so happy to have a little girl! Jason was
disappointed; his desire for all sons was already thwarted. Ryan's
babyhood had been a baptism of fire for me; he had colic for three
months straight, with bloody stools and never-ending wailing.
Aleena proved to be a content baby and very pretty in her bonnets
and flounced dresses that I sewed for her.

*   *   *

Jason was a demanding husband; he insisted upon obedience and
he wanted things done his way. If I was good, he took care of me
when I was sick and bought me things I needed. He might bring
me chocolate or, rarely, wild flowers he had picked on the side of
the road. It was like finding water in a parched desert and always
amazed me when he did those things. One night, when I was asleep
in bed with baby Aleena off to my side, Jason suddenly screamed,
sat up, and put his fist through the wall next to the bed. As I gazed
in shock at the hole the next morning, I realized it could have been

my face. Previously, he had dislocated my nose in a similar accident.

In addition, he did not like me to visit my family and needed to approve of my friends. I had to wear my hair and clothes the way *he* liked and agree with him on *his* political and religious views. It was his right, as the man of the house, to control me, and he would take no backtalk or attitude. He warned me that I was not to have an attitude like my mother did toward my father—despite the fact that my parents loved and respected each other. There were lots of rules to follow, the foremost being that I could never say "no" to him.

A Trip to Idaho

Jason's fantasy world was taking him down the survivalist road. "Hard times are coming. The government is corrupt, and we need to think survival."

When baby Aleena was about a year old, Jason decided to take our little family on a trip to Idaho. He and his older brother Keith (the one to whom I had tried to give the Cracker Jack toy) had bought fifteen acres of land in Idaho a few years before I met Jason. It was to be their refuge from society, a place where they could live off the land and be mountain men. We readied Jason's '64 Chevy short-bed truck for the trip. It was so high off the ground that I needed help getting into it. A mattress was put in the back and a tarp pulled over the truck bed on a framework. I sewed the unwieldy canvas on my treadle machine using a large needle.

While I was very excited to see someplace new, my brain must have been on autopilot. That a normal girl from a happy family could be brainwashed into such nonsense is appalling to me now. I wore prairie dresses and aprons, Mary Jane shoes and even bonnets! It was the 1980s, for heaven's sake! Jason had guns hidden in the truck and wore mountain-man gear, as did his brother and friends. My younger brother, Sam, also decked out like a backwoodsman came along on the trip, as did my little sister, Jacquie, who helped me with the babies. She paid no attention to the nonsense.

We drove a thousand miles to see Jason's land in Idaho. When we got there, Keith brought in a well driller and had a well drilled as we camped nearby.

Jason's idea was to live off the land in a tent. The temperature plummeted to thirty below zero in that area every winter for a spell, but he felt we could tough it out. He relayed this information as he walked toward me, pulling out his penis to pee on the ground in front of the babies. I held baby Aleena while Ryan toddled beside me, embarrassed that he would be so crude in front of our children.

The land was remote enough that you couldn't walk to town but close enough so that it didn't take too long in a vehicle. I still didn't drive, which meant that I would be isolated. The last time I had revisited the subject of getting my license, Jason told me to forget it— he was sure that I would kill myself and the children. He believed that all women should stay off the road; it was women on the road that caused the accidents. Another time, he told me I was unfit to drive, all of which fed my fear of driving. That sinking feeling in the pit of my stomach told me that he must know what he is talking about, that I must not be normal, like other people.

There's something wrong with me, I often thought with great sadness. There *was* something wrong with me: I did not have strong boundaries, and had poor self-esteem, which Jason carefully cultivated. I realize now that when a person has strong boundaries and great self-esteem, they won't allow anyone to control them.

I just couldn't see myself and my babies stuck in a tent in the middle of nowhere, especially during thirty-below-zero weather. *What was he thinking?* But I knew that it was what he had always wanted to do—live away from civilization, in isolation, with no electricity or bills except maybe taxes. He didn't like people. I had entered into his dream, and it was becoming my nightmare.

* * *

During the trip, the truck broke down near a small town called Aldridge, population of around 300 souls. It was located in the mountains about half an hour's drive south of the Idaho property.

We hobbled the truck to a small park by the city's water tower and then looked around. The town had a main street with a couple of markets, a pharmacy, post office, library, hardware store, three small restaurants, and a school. There was even a small auto shop, which was good, because Jason needed parts to fix the truck. Aldridge was on the main north-south highway in western Idaho, so it catered to tourists. It was also the last town before fishermen trekked off on Highway 81 northwest to Turnstile Dam and the Rand River. The whole area was incredibly beautiful.

We camped with the children in the tower park while Jason, Keith, and Sam fixed the truck. Jacqui helped me with the babies. She was a young teen, and the trip was an adventure for her. My brother Sam fit right in with the men. He had an old tattered mountain-man hat on and wore worn jeans, lace-up boots, and a button-up plaid over his T-shirt.

Across from the park was an old white clapboard and green-trimmed house. It looked neglected and abandoned, with broken windows and an overgrown, weedy lawn. At around 105 years old, it was one of the oldest houses in town. The ancient structure had a half-hipped roof, peeling paint, and worn siding. There was a screen-enclosed upper porch and an open lower front porch lifted by one of the maples in the front yard. The grand-daddy maples were almost as old as the house, as evidenced by their great girth and majesty.

Convincing Jason to buy the house was a major hurdle, and I'm not quite sure how I did it, but it was imperative if I wanted to avoid living in a tent with my sweet babies. By asking around town, I finally found the owner. He was happy to sell the neglected house, since it had been sitting abandoned for years. A bargain was struck for us to make payments, and when we finally headed south back home to California, we were buying an old neglected house instead of a tent. It amazes me now, as I write this story, that at the time, I didn't realize that changing my story started with changing my actions. I could have passively accepted living in a tent, but, instead, I found a way around it. My actions changed my future. I only wish that I had been more proactive and aware.

The house needed major work. The main part of the house sat on a few rows of bricks, which was considered a foundation, back when it was built. The roof had leaked for years, the plumbing and electrical had to be redone, the plaster was falling off the lath, the floors were worn, and the kitchen had no foundation so it sagged back to the earth. However, none of that scared me. I knew that Jason had the skills to refurbish the old house, and I would help him. I enjoyed that kind of work and loved learning new skills. I also very much wanted my own home.

If I had any idea how much my children and I would suffer in that house, I never would have agreed to go back to Idaho. To me, though, after living in borrowed homes, dumpy trailers, a warehouse filled with mice, and narrowly avoiding a tent in sub-zero winter, I was excited… *my own home*! Jason was happy to be making some progress on getting me away from my family, and besides, Idaho was filled with conservatives. In his opinion, it was a good idea to get out of California before it got any more liberal. There had also been some drive-by shootings in Jason's home town, which added to his belief that it was unsafe to rear children in California. Unbelievably, I went along with that line of reasoning.

ISOLATION AND DESOLATION—
MOVING TO IDAHO

Overhead, I could see the underbelly of the hot truck. I inhaled the smell of baked asphalt, engine oil, and the elusive scent that signals the close of day. My babies snuggled, one on each side of my pregnant belly. Exhausted, they barely stirred.

WHEN WE LEFT CALIFORNIA TO MOVE TO IDAHO—after months of getting rid of things and saying goodbye to our families—I was five months pregnant with our third child. Three heavily laden trucks made the trip that time. One was driven by my brother Sam. Another was driven by Jason's brother Keith, with Jed, one of the banjo players from my brother's band, as his passenger. The third was Jason's old camo-painted truck with our two babies seated on the far side of the cab and me in the middle. On the trip north, after the first long, exhausting day, the trucks signaled each other and pulled off the side of the highway. It was August, and, although the sun had set, the terrible heat persisted. I was very tired and had been longing to stop and lie down for some time. It was cramped and muggy in the truck, and I didn't have much room to move. The babies were asleep in their car seats with their little necks kinked, even though I kept trying to prop them up.

After a quick consult, the men began to throw old woolen blankets and sleeping bags down out of the truck beds and onto the side of the highway.

Really? You've got to be kidding! I thought to myself.

They spread the bedding partly under the jacked-up truck. It was good to lie prone after so many hours in the baking truck without air conditioning. We had been keeping the heater on full-bore in the truck in order to cool down the engine, as it tended to overheat on the long, high mountain passes. Having hot air blowing in your face on a scorching day isn't fun for anyone, much less small children captive in their car seats or someone who is five months pregnant.

Glancing up, I could see the underbelly of the hot truck as I inhaled the smell of baked asphalt, engine oil, and the elusive scent that signals the close of day. My babies snuggled, one on each side of my pregnant belly. Worn out, they barely stirred. We lay with our heads sticking part way out from beneath the vehicle. As dusk settled, the last rays of the setting sun quietly slipped away. The summer night's warmth held me captive while heat from the truck, weariness, and dehydration took its toll. I fell into an uneasy sleep, disturbed by the roaring trucks and cars that raced by in the darkness just a few feet away. As I drifted off, a thought occurred to me... *My mother never had to sleep under a car on the side of the road—my father never would have allowed that.*

* * *

After two seemingly endless days, we arrived back in Aldridge. It was the dog days of summer, and the heat was oppressive. We set up camp in the house. There were no mattresses to sleep on, although we did bring some antique dressers and a bedframe with us. We were without electricity or refrigeration, but there was a roof over our heads, and Jason was able to turn on the water.

We got to work immediately, cleaning out years of dirt and filth. Broken windows were repaired, stained floors scrubbed, and spider webs cleared away as we tried to make the old house a home. Immediately, the neighbors noticed the activity in the once-abandoned house. Our motley group was warmly welcomed and given donations of clothes, blankets, and a mattress. We seemed to have made the grade of being "deserving poor." The sheriff stopped in to question us, as no one had seen inhabitants in the house for over a decade, and some of the locals wondered if we were squatters.

Ryan and Aleena shared a sleeping bag, which I laid out in the front room, near our recently donated mattress. Outside, grasshoppers shot out of the high, dry weeds; they were everywhere, making their clacking sounds. They clawed up my legs, under my dress, and spat tobacco-like juice on the calico. Crickets sang their song, and no-see-ums bit me deeply on my neck as I hung up cold, hand-washed diapers on a hastily-strung rope in the fresh morning air. This was the summer of my life: I was still in my twenties, young, strong—and pregnant—again.

After clearing out the spiders and broken glass, I scrubbed the dirt out of the vintage bathtub and filled it with cold water. We only had cold running water, as the water heater was broken. Since it was so hot outside, I figured a cold bath would feel good for sweaty bodies. I tried to bathe the babies, but as soon as they were in the water, they gasped, screamed, and stood up quickly. I poured water over them and tried to clean them, but they were anxious to get out. Their lips were blue and their teeth chattered as I rubbed them dry. It astonished me. *Was it that cold?*

I bundled the babies up in blankets and let them snuggle on the mattress together to get warm, then proceeded to take a bath myself. As soon as the sensitive skin along my ribs slid into the cold water, I gasped in shock. Then I understood why my babies wanted out so fast! The clear mountain water was runoff from high snowpack. It was some of the purest, sweetest-tasting water anywhere, and it was *icy* cold, even in August. I chided the reluctant men; they weren't tough enough to take a cold bath.

The locusts trilled their haunting sound throughout the day, and the roasted smell of sunburnt weeds reminded me of baked bread. The huge granddaddy maple trees towering over the house provided dense shade so the interior was cool enough if we kept the doors and windows shut. A camp stove set up on the kitchen counter enabled me to boil up some fat ears of corn we'd bought from a local u-pick-'em farm. That was the first meal in our new home, and, because we didn't have a table or chairs yet, I laid out dinner on the newly scrubbed kitchen floor, using chipped enamel camping plates. We all gathered around—our little family, our family members, and the friends who helped us with the long move—and gave thanks. The salty, buttery goodness of freshly picked corn and icy mountain water filled us with contentment after a hard day of work.

The ceiling in the main part of the house reached a lofty height of twelve feet. The windows were tall and also reached down low, almost like two windows stacked one on top of the other. Plaster-covered lath walls layered with decades of peeling, flaking paint over a sturdy framework made up the main part of the house. There was a pervasive smell of age, of something old and careworn, like the odor of ancient wood in an old museum. Although it leaked when it rained and there were years of rot under the roof upstairs, there was no smell of mold or dankness in the main section. That part of the house seemed dry.

We discovered old, brittle newspapers that had been used for insulation and tucked into the spaces between the walls. Some of them were dated 1905. One of the neighbor's children, searching for treasure under the front porch, dragged out an ancient pair of hand-stitched lady's bloomers, intact after so many long years. An old brown doctor's bag was found in the shed. We also noticed that bees had made a hive inside one of the outer walls but had abandoned it ages ago, leaving dry, hard honeycomb under the wood siding. A rumor circulated around town that a box of coins and metal slugs had been buried under the house by the boy who originally lived there. We were living in an old house with buried treasure...! What more could you ask for?

* * *

Jason discovered the local dump.

One of his first dump finds was a discarded washing machine, he brought it home, fixed it, and set it up outside. I hung the wet clothes on a rope strung between trees on the side yard. The smell of fresh, sun-dried clothes was one of the sweetest smells; I would bury my nose in the laundry and inhale the scent of mountain air.

He replaced an element on the water heater, and we were finally able to have hot baths, but I continued to use cold water to wash clothes in the washer, which we set up out back of the house.

He also set up an old electric range in the kitchen, also a dump-find. The oven part of the range was only big enough to bake one loaf of bread at a time. Eventually, most of our furnishings and appliances were dump finds or donations. We paid thirty dollars for a water-stained king-size mattress that had been patched on one side.

The house had many old fixtures. Turning on a light meant pushing a button instead of flipping a switch. The babies were fond of climbing on a chair and pushing the buttons to turn the lights off and on, when they could get away with it. There were glass and stamped-metal doorknobs, and the windows had cords embedded in the jambs along tracks to move them up and down. I nicknamed them the guillotine windows after one of them let loose and slammed down on both of my wrists. Thankfully, the window edges were flat and not sharp, or I would not be typing this story.

The kitchen had a tilt-out wood box under the window that could

be filled with kindling from the outside and then tilted inward for access from the kitchen. In years gone by, it had fed a wood-fired stove for cooking and heating. The plumbing leaked below the double porcelain kitchen sink that sat on a white metal cabinet; a rusty mess of corroded metal flaked off the cabinet in layers. The dry wall on the kitchen ceiling hung down dangerously in places; by peeking through the gaps, you could see sky through the roof over the kitchen, which let the rain in. It stayed that way several years, with plaster dust, spiders, and dirt falling onto the kitchen table. I finally tore it all down myself. Once exposed, the old ceiling boards looked much nicer.

We shared a single bathroom, but its tile floor had crumbled and the rotted old underlayment showed through in places. It had a vintage pedestal sink and bathtub; their porcelain glaze was worn off. Even with the neglect of years, there was a certain wonder about the ancient house, a feeling of stepping into the past, smelling its scent, and experiencing a bygone era.

Winter Child

He taunted me by inching closer to the bed as I labored. My face was turned away, but I could feel his presence. I cried out to him to stop as he slowly reached his hand toward my bed to see if I would say anything.

It had been four months since we moved into our old Idaho mountain home. Our family members had long since made the trip back to California. Time drew near for me to give birth for the third time. I bore this baby with much anguish on one of the coldest nights of the year, with overnight temperatures in the single digits.

I had not received prenatal care, nor did I have a doctor. My water broke at home, and I labored all day long. Still, the baby did not come. Then, the water turned green. The ambulance arrived, and, with assistance, I wobbled out on the snow, leaking amniotic fluid along the way before crawling into the back of the vehicle.

The emergency personnel took me to a little backwards clinic located near the bottom of the mountain. The clinic's medical practices were a bit behind the times. They didn't even know that pubic shaving and episiotomies were no longer automatically used for births. I don't believe the old doctor had kept up with the advances in medicine.

Labor was very hard, and Jason's presence nearby caused me to suffer during contractions. My spirit became sensitive to his negative vibes and rough manner, and I begged him to give me some space during contractions. He taunted me by inching closer to the bed as I labored. I turned my face away, but I could feel his presence. I cried out to him to stop as he slowly reached his hand toward my bed to see if I would say anything. The birth finally drew near. Jason intervened, as the doctor, who was determined to give me an episiotomy, readied his scalpel.

"You cut her, and I cut you," Jason said with cold determination.

He scared the doctor, and I wasn't cut. It was my third child, and I had no need of an episiotomy. Most of my babies had nice round unmolded heads at birth, so I seemed to be fashioned correctly to have babies. Our new son, Alex, was born covered in meconium; he had also inhaled it and needed better medical care than the clinic could provide. Early the next morning, after a few hours of recuperation, I crawled into Jason's truck with our new baby, and we headed to the nearest hospital, another half an hour down the snowy roads. When we arrived, the attendant asked me if I needed a wheelchair.

I looked at him in a daze, confused. "I just had a baby. I am exhausted."

Since I had been transported to the clinic in an ambulance, I had no clothes, except for the nightgown I was wearing when I left home. I didn't even own a robe. So Jason took me home that night, and I left my newborn son in the hospital alone. It was what was expected. I am not sure why Jason didn't just return the following day and bring me some clothes—I was expected to go home with him, and so I did. My other two children had been taken in by the townsfolk before the ambulance arrived. They were being cared for by people I had met in church. Although they seemed nice and owned the store in town, they were strangers to me and my little ones.

The sharp edge of reality came up and hit me hard in the chest. It felt like my heart had been torn out of me when I had to leave my sick newborn. I knew my other children must have been scared, too, being suddenly thrust into the arms of strangers—though I was very grateful to these wonderful people for stepping in to care for my babies. I was in a state of emotional shock, not to mention post-partum depression.

As darkness approached, we drove home slowly on the winding, ice-crusted roads. When we arrived, I opened the door to a freezing house; it had been unheated since we left. The one old woodstove didn't heat for long, if it wasn't gorging on wood continuously. Being a California girl, I wasn't used to the low temperatures. I had never lived in snow country or had to deal with stoking a fire or traversing frozen roads. There was no real insulation in the ancient house to hold in warmth either.

The shock of being fresh from a very hard childbirth, missing my other children, and coming back to a frigid house was too much. I bundled up, crawled into an icy bed, and waited for the reluctant morning sun to cast soft shadows in the room. It was too cold to sleep; I shivered uncontrollably under chilly blankets and stared into the darkness. When the morning light filtered through the window shade, I glanced over at Jason as he slept next to me. I was shocked. His mustache was *fully iced over*, and dragon vapor shot from his lips.

It would take two days to rewarm the house.

I returned to the hospital the following day and stayed with my new baby, Alex, as he recovered from pneumonia. After a week of medical care, we brought him home. The temperature had fallen below zero during the time I spent in the warm, cozy hospital, which made it that much harder to return to a chilly uncomfortable house. But I was anxious to see my toddlers and missed them something fierce.

During the previous summer, when we first arrived at the old house, Jason had removed the various woodstoves scattered around the house, except for the one in the dining room. There had been one in the kitchen, another in the back bedroom, and evidence that, long ago, a small wood burner had been used upstairs. The last remaining heat source was an ancient Monarch with brown enamel on the outside and firebrick lining the interior. It smoked and did not heat well. Most of the heat shot up the stovepipe. A few ceiling fans helped to distribute what little heat there was. The door to the stairwell was kept closed to keep the heat from rushing upstairs.

At first, Jason used some coal lumps we found in the back shed to make the fire really hot, but after the first winter, we discovered that the lath on the near wall and the wood flooring got too hot and dry. The old parched floorboards began to splinter; the plaster cracked and fell off the wall. The heat from the fire caused cold drafts to circulate from the rest of the house. A simmering pot of water kept on top of the stove wasn't enough to humidify the parched air. Throats and noses dried out, and hair flew wild with static sparking. The house was intensely cold.

I wore snow boots in the house and several layers under my dress, plus a jacket and long underwear. However, my feet froze in the boots, causing nerve damage in my toes. (It would take over a decade for the nerves to heal.) A bowl of water placed on the kitchen floor in the evening turned to solid ice by morning. Since there was no foundation under that part of the house and the underwood had rotted away, the floor sloped as it sagged back towards the earth. I tried to keep the kids out of the kitchen when the temperature plummeted.

The old wooden floors throughout the house were dry and splinters got embedded into the children's feet and hands.

Our back bedroom, where Jason and I slept, was so far from the heat that I kept my winter jacket on in bed and wound a woolen scarf around my head at night. Layers of blankets were heaped on the bed like a leaden weight. It was an ugly room with warped floorboards and unfinished walls. Jason put a fan over the bed to circulate air, and in the summer, when it was very hot, he kept the fan on high all night long.

*   *   *

Eventually, Jason fixed the front porch and removed one of the large ancient maples whose roots were lifting the porch.

I was sad about that. "Goodbye, grandpa tree."

Removing the bent tree did improve the appearance of the place, though, and allowed more light into the dark house. He also repaired some of the broken plaster and lath. Then I painted the living room a warm peach color.

The steep roofline was a half-hip style and the upper story had dormers on the side facing the street. In a later winter, when the boys were older, they opened the dormer windows and slid down the roof onto the snow, which had piled all the way up to the roofline. In that same winter, some of the roofs of old houses in town caved in from the heavy weight of the snow.

* * *

During our second winter in our mountain home, the studded snow tires were stolen out of the back shed, so we were snowbound that whole winter. We couldn't drive anywhere as long as the roads were icy. I bought groceries from the little store in town, which was only two blocks away, and hauled them home. We ate poorly and were always hungry; we were living on beans, rice, potatoes, and sometimes a stew made from free kidneys I begged from the butcher.

The butcher always teased, "Make sure you boil the piss out of 'em."

That winter we were constantly irritable and cold—always cold. The kids and I could never seem to get warm. In the spring, like a visiting angel, the former owner of the house brought over two bags of groceries, including orange juice and bananas. Never had anything tasted so good! It was a shock to the senses.

I decided to try and get government help to feed the children. Jason agreed to food assistance but put his foot down about any other help. So we got government surplus food once a month; it made a big difference in our diet and morale. Government surplus at that time included butter, cheese, beans, and cornmeal.

We were poverty-stricken and had not paid the mortgage for a long time. The first full year we lived in Aldridge, Jason made $2,000 doing odd jobs around town. The government surplus was not enough. The following year, at my insistence, we also applied for food stamps. But Jason refused any monetary help, even though we were eligible for it, so the mortgage went unpaid.

The people of the town knew we were poor and struggling to feed our growing brood. The kindly folk helped out when they could although, at times, it could be a challenge to accept their gifts charitably. One day, a knock sounded on the front door. An elderly woman and her adult son were outside, and I welcomed them in. They had a problem. The woman wanted to clean out her old freezer and restock it with new groceries but felt guilty about throwing away all of that "good food." I realized that some of the older people thought that way as a result of the Great Depression years, when their own parents and grandparents had gone hungry.

My heart sank when I saw what the boxes contained. I tried to be gracious and thanked them as they left with the satisfaction that they were "sharing with the poor." Then I promptly got a large garbage bag and did what she should have done: I threw it all away. The food was years' old, outdated, freezer-burned, and not fit for consumption. That was why *she* had wanted to get rid of it.

> *"I recall one exceptionally cold winter when my dad, a few siblings, and I went out to get a Christmas tree way up in the mountains. After a while, my feet and hands started to sting with pain from the cold. I started to cry and begged my dad to go, but he just told me to suck it up and act like a man about it. I ended up getting minor frostbite and nerve damage. Even to this day, if I get somewhat cold, anything warm burns like hot coals."*
> —*Excerpt from* My Life *by Alex Gannon*

During the summer, I tried several times to have a garden in the backyard. It was a challenge, because there were only about six inches of soil over a layer of hard-packed river rock. Although we were near the top of the mountain, it seemed as, if in the distant past, it had been river bottom. The hard layer was very thick, but a pickax taken to it would soon yield water. Since the water was so close to the surface, the huge trees were able to grow and thrive on such thin soil, once their roots finally made their way through the densely packed layer of rock.

When it got too warm, the children slept upstairs in the screened-in porch. Summers were very hot, but often, in the evenings, thunderstorms and lightning rolled in. The storms offered some relief from the heat, but they also contributed to the next day's humidity.

A storm in the mountains could be an awe-inspiring event.

Usually, the whole family would sit on the porch and watch it approach. You could feel the pressure overhead and hear distant sounds as if they were close by. There would be a pause before the wind kicked up, and then lightning cracked across the sky like a gunshot, followed by a pelting, heavy rain. Then, for a time, the oppressive heat was replaced by a welcomed coolness and the gentle, joyous smell of rain vapor as it emanated from the earth.

*   *   *

When fall rolled around, I gathered my three children and as many rakes as I could find, and we raked the thick layer of maple leaves into heaps. I knew the neighbors didn't like the heavy layer of leaves carpeting our yard. Once the wind started to blow, those leaves wouldn't honor proper boundaries. The smell of autumn permeated the outdoors—dampness, smoky chimneys, and the burning leaves in neighboring yards. The crisp air had an invigorating feel to it. We had several mounds going when the inevitable happened. The rakes were tossed aside, and, with arms and legs flailing, the children raced each other and buried themselves into the fluffy piles. *Oh well, nature's blanket would be good for the lawn and protect the big-daddy maples' roots.* Very pregnant with my fourth child, I smiled as I watched them.

The discarded claw foot kitchen stove sat in a corner of the porch, littered with leaves, dust and a pile of firewood. With curved legs and a white porcelain exterior, it looked the part of an antique but was just a sham. It had not lived up to the practicalities of baking for a growing family, so Jason had found another more modern oven at the dump and brought it home. Aleena played house with the shamed outcast oven in the corner of the porch, baking a small "cake" in it. Two-year-old Alex kept pestering her. He felt the mud was done baking and wanted to taste it. As he tried to open the door, she wrestled to slam it shut.

A bloodcurdling scream is enough to give any mother a heart attack. With my nine-months-pregnant belly slowing me down only a little, I flung open the front door to see my two-year-old son screaming in terror as his little hand dripped blood: a thumbnail had been torn off. I screamed at Aleena, who looked shell-shocked, and chaos ensued. Someone contacted the doctor; I was sitting on a step at the bottom of our long front walk, holding Alex's bloody hand, when the doctor came by. The wound was raw, with the nail hanging by a thread of flesh. My son whimpered in my lap while Aleena went and hid in her room, feeling rightly that she had been blamed unjustly for an accident.

The doctor seemed more concerned for me than the lost nail. I was blanched and too calm. It was a terrible fault—I got very angry when one of my babies was hurt. Being hormonal at the end of pregnancy didn't help.

I remember my own mother, burdened by twelve children, crying her heart out with gut-wrenching sobs behind the closed door of her bedroom after she'd screamed at us for being normal, selfish brats. Cowering and crying real tears, we would go clean our rooms or something equally noble in order to assuage our guilt.

How desperately I loved my mother. She was always so patient and sweet, but it was difficult for her to show her emotions or be affectionate. She had been emotionally abused as a child. With the help of my therapist decades later, I realized that I continued to search for her attention and love by choosing emotionally unavailable men. The roots of abuse are deep and long-lasting, often reaching through the generations to poison many lives.

*   *   *

As time went by, the old house became a storage place for the junk that Jason dragged home from the local landfill. He furnished the house, fixed broken refrigerators, dryers, washers, stoves, and even lawn mowers, all of which he'd scavenged. The shed was packed from top to bottom with anything that might be of use *someday*. There were mowers, appliances, and car parts in heaps, and all kinds of things piled high in boxes and strewn all over the place in a messy fashion.

As time went by, Jason became a hoarder. He took comfort in

knowing that, if he needed it someday, it was available, although the space left for living dwindled. One summer, when my parents made the long trip to Aldridge to visit, my dad was astonished when Jason promptly took him dump diving, "to have fun."

More Catholic than the Pope

At first, our growing family attended the small Catholic church a few blocks away. Jason often fought with the priests over rules and regulations. One of the priests refused to baptize our baby, and we had to wait a year for the child to be baptized in another church. Jason and I fought over his forcing me to wear a hat to church. He felt women should have their head covered in a place of worship. I also didn't see any harm in holding hands with people in church for the "Our Father" or receiving communion from a woman, but I didn't dare go against Jason. The pre-Vatican church was the *true* church, according to Jason, and the modern church had become a travesty.

Holding hands with other people during the "Our Father" was a sin, according to Jason's way of thinking. To me, refusing an old woman's outstretched hand in the spirit of superior obedience was a lack of charity and love. Once, when I accidentally got in the wrong line and received communion from a woman, Jason raged at me all the way home, in front of the children. When I realized my mistake, I was fearful but decided to stay in the line rather than make a scene. I knew I would be in trouble later.

Weary of Jason's fantasy of reenacting the frontier days, I stopped wearing long, old-fashioned prairie dresses. I was done playing that game, embarrassed that people often assumed I was Amish or Mormon when that wasn't the case. I still had to wear a dress or skirt; Jason would not allow me to wear pants, and it upset him that I did not want to wear a hat in church. He wore whatever he wanted and went wherever he pleased.

When I brought that fact up to him, he gestured at his clothes and replied, "This *is* what you want me to wear."

* * *

One evening, the light streamed from the upper church window and bathed our little family in a soft glow as we sat on folding chairs in the very back of the church, well behind the pews. I had dutifully perched a straw hat festooned with ribbons and flowers on my head and wore a three-tiered pink dress draped over my pregnant stomach that reached well below my knees.

"I see you are *real* Catholics," said a whiskered man, who smiled and gestured toward my hat as he entered the church's rear door. His heavyset wife followed him with a cowboy hat covering her grey locks. They were "fellow sympathizers," "ultra" Catholics. I nodded my head toward him but said nothing.

If he only knew... I thought, remembering the time my husband tried to force me to wear a couch afghan on my head after a frantic scramble to find my missing hat...

"Where's your head covering?" Jason demanded.

I was afraid, because I really didn't know where it was and knew he would think I was lying.

"I don't know. It's lost and I can't find it. I've looked everywhere," I replied, feeling guilty even though I was telling the truth.

He rummaged around frantically, searching for the missing hat. It was late and we needed to leave if we were going to make it to church on time.

I went out to get in the car; the children were already buckled in. I didn't dare say anything for fear of provoking his anger. Soon after, he came running out with an afghan in his hands.

"Better to look ridiculous than offend God," he said triumphantly while waving it towards me.

Flabbergasted, I refused; it was absurd to even imagine wearing a couch afghan on my head. That was the beginning of many fights between us over the subject of wearing a head covering in church.

In desperation, Jason finally drove me to the Squaw Valley Hermitage one day, demanding that the priest inform me that I *had* to obey my husband.

The priest looked at Jason oddly then replied, "A husband and wife should mutually respect each other."

After that, Jason left me alone, and I quit wearing head coverings to church altogether.

Even though he wanted his family to follow the old rules of the church, Jason was never strict with himself. He did not follow the old ways or wear a suit and tie to church.

He became embittered at the locals for going along with the "heretical" priests in the small parish. Our family went to any length to avoid going along with "heresy," which included anything that did not meet with Jason's approval about the church and dogma. We were becoming more Catholic than the pope. He became known in the community for being eccentric, arrogant, and demanding.

And so, to avoid other heretical parishioners, we began the challenging trek to the hermitage very early on Sunday mornings.

At that time of year, it was very dark and the temperature in our house was below freezing. During the night, the fire in the woodstove died down and it was bitterly cold. We all used many layers of blankets to keep warm, but getting up when it was so cold was a shock to the system.

Reluctantly, I woke them one by one. "Hurry, get dressed warmly, and put your snow boots on," I whispered to the children.

It was very hard for me to get the babies up and ready in time to make the 6:00 a.m. mass, especially when the roads were snow-covered or frozen over. In the wee hours of the morning, they snuggled beneath blankets in the cold car as it crunched through drifts of hardened snow on the winding road. The hermitage had a small chapel for the few nuns who lived there and only a half dozen seats with kneelers. I bundled the smaller children in the back on the chapel floor and let them sleep through the service, sprawled out with limbs entangled.

> *I only remember fragments of my life because it was*
> *traumatic to me, and I chose to forget things as they*
> *happened. I vaguely recall bits and pieces as far back as*

possibly five years of age.

I was raised in a large, old house in Aldridge, Idaho. I can still see my mom and older brother tearing old plaster and other various decaying parts of the house away, as they were dangerous and falling apart. I was too young at the time to be of much help. To this day, however, I remember how cold I was all the time. My hands and feet were always senseless with the cold; the only source of heat was one wood stove in the lower portion of the house which did little to nothing, given the fact that there was no insulation in the house.

Also, my two brothers and I slept upstairs, which had plaster and lead paint falling off the walls onto our beds. The small amount of heat from the wood stove never reached as far as upstairs, so we spent our entire existence there freezing and chilled to the bone. Besides the never-ending chill, the floors were old, splintering wood. I remember constantly getting huge slivers of wood buried deep into my cold numb flesh.

—*Excerpt from* My Life *by Alex Gannon, third child of Tessy and Jason Gannon*

A New Son

Once I watched in fascination as a cat fought a praying mantis on the front porch. The praying mantis won, and the cat ran away. Sometimes, the little guy wins if they stand their ground. You need courage to stand your ground.

My fourth child, a son we named Brent, was born with a smile on his face. He was small, sickly, and low on iron. I had nursed all of my babies but hoped I could start tracking my cycles and using the Natural Family Planning Method to avoid another pregnancy again so soon. Exhaustion and depression weighed me down, and I knew

I had to do something. I felt a sense of despair about having no control over my situation, so I got a calendar and started tracking my menstrual cycles. I also tried to put the baby on formula, but Brent didn't do well with it, so the doctor switched him to soy formula; he seemed to be very allergic to cow's milk. Brent grew up to have a multitude of intestinal troubles, allergies, and other problems, possibly from being switched to formula. I often regretted not nursing him longer and felt selfish for putting my needs before the needs of my child. I didn't realize how much Brent would suffer from my decision.

I loved getting out for walks. I found a vintage baby carriage with large wheels and often had a baby and a toddler in it, while the older children trailed along. We walked to the post office, the store, the library, or just around town. Once, when I got away by myself for a while—which wasn't often—I made my way to the cemetery outside of town and wandered along, looking at the gravestones. I felt sad when I noticed that some of them were for babies who had died.

Along one side of the cemetery was a whole row of children buried next to each other, all from the same family. Curious, I asked one of the locals what had happened to the family. It seemed the mother of the family, like most mothers of that generation, canned her own food from the family garden. She served canned beets for dinner, and the children ate them then they all got sick and died of botulism poisoning. I never forgot that story; it was enough to keep me from canning any low-acid food. Instead, I canned peaches, elderberry syrup, jams, jellies, applesauce, and apple pie filling, but no beets, meat, or green beans. I still won't eat someone else's home-canned, low-acid food.

The library was only a few blocks away; it was another place I could escape to by myself once in a while. If I went alone anywhere, I knew that Jason would invariably show up to make sure I was there. Although he pretended he just happened to be going by, I knew he was checking up on me. It made him nervous and uncomfortable whenever I went anywhere by myself. He was jealous and suspicious that other men might be looking at me and needed to know where I was, who I was with, and what I was doing.

> *I would always give my parents a hug and kiss before going to bed. My mom was always eager to show her love to me. Sometime at around the age of four or five, I remember one night going to bid my parents goodnight, and my father refused to hug me. I was devastated and couldn't understand why he would turn me away. He told me that I was too old to show affection and that it wasn't "manly" to hug other guys. Words absolutely **cannot** describe the way my heart sank and the degree to which I hurt inside after that moment in my life. To this day, at 26 years old, I still cry over that one memory.*
> —*Excerpt from* My Life *by Alex Gannon*

Once, I watched in fascination as a cat fought a praying mantis on the front porch. The praying mantis won, and the cat ran away. Sometimes, the little guy wins if they stand their ground. But you need courage to stand your ground.

I mowed the lawn until my eldest son was old enough to take over the job. The children and I raked the leaves in the fall, and I watched them jump in the piles with happy squeals. Sewing clothes to keep the kids warm kept me busy. But they were still bothered by chilblains (tissue damage from freezing) on their arms and hands. The adults and older children hauled in firewood and chopped kindling, if the pile got low. Garbage was often piled high against the wall in my kitchen that once had a kindling box attached to it; the pile stank and leaked on the kitchen floor. Or it was heaped up outside in the truck bed until Jason was ready to haul it to away. He did not like taking the trash out. I took it out for a while and realized one day that the more I did, the less he did. So I quit taking it out, but I had to suffer with the terrible smell. When the boys were old enough, they took over the job.

*   *   *

Jason didn't want any of us to brush our teeth or use floss. It was his conviction that brushing made teeth decay and flossing drove the food down into the gums. He would not allow me to use deodorant either, much to my embarrassment, although, in later years, he relented once he needed to use it to be presentable at work.

Once I tried to be normal and dragged out an old pair of pants to wear to the river for a picnic with some neighbors. That pushed Jason's comfort level too far. He was upset and told me I looked ugly in pants, that my butt was too flat. He wanted me to dress to please him, and he didn't like me in pants. I was not permitted to cut or style my hair, either. I was to let it grow long, and he was the only one allowed to trim it. He liked me with a small braid on one side and a clip with flowers or a ribbon in my hair. It didn't matter what I liked. I hated my hair. It was bedraggled due to rarely being trimmed, and it made me look dumpy, which Jason seemed to like.

At times, I found myself thinking like he did, agreeing with him and even making decisions like him. Later, after I fell apart, I realized that I had, in many ways, *become* like him. Slowly, his boundaries engulfed my own until one day I had none. His rules were my rules, his thoughts were my thoughts, his wants and desires were lived out in me. Except for a tiny voice still deep within, I became lost. Swimming upstream sapped my energy, and I began to give in and give up. I dared not think differently than he did, or I would pay for it. The small place of defiance left within me annoyed him; he knew it was there—that disobedient, independent person hidden inside. For the most part, though, I complied; my brainwashing was complete—or at least he assumed so.

Of *course* I would enjoy poverty, being continually pregnant, living without comforts, a virtual prisoner in my own home, enduring subpar housing, taking on his political and religious views, wearing dresses, and not using deodorant. Surely anyone with brains could see that caring for teeth caused cavities! Besides, everyone knew that men were superior to women, white males were the dominant race, and Jason was more intelligent than other people.

His way was best. His way was the only way.

* * *

Jason was a master at manipulating, twisting the truth, and instilling fear. He could lie so well that people would believe him, even if they had witnessed the truth. If he wanted to force you to believe something, he carefully and methodically twisted bits of information and implanted doubts until you were finally brainwashed. If you still resisted him, he started to play emotional guilt games and used intimidation. He was extremely intelligent, and he used it, together with lying, to control those around him.

Because Jason's father had had a terrible temper (perhaps he felt overburdened with his large family, once his children were gone, he became a gentle soul), Jason would not tolerate any show of temper or irritability from his wife. He had a way of pouting, sulking, or becoming dark and stony if things didn't go his way. I tried with great effort to be the perfect wife he wanted so he would love me, but the effort of being perfect often left me peevish. At times, I got tired and became cranky and irritable, I yelled at the kids or lost my temper. It was hard, holding everything together. Sometimes I just wanted to be selfish and do whatever I wanted. Being stuck indoors and unable to drive anywhere was particularly hard, especially in winter. I was convinced that I was a terrible failure, a bad person, an imperfect wife. I had no self-esteem and it showed.

I didn't realize then that Jason *could not love*. He was incapable of emotional attachment; I would find out later that he was most likely a sociopath and a narcissist. I became discouraged, depressed, and sad as the years wore on. I resigned myself to living in a bad marriage under desperate circumstances. I felt that God demanded it of me. Vows were serious business, and I meant to keep my word to God... for better or for worse. Although, if I had thought about it, I did *not* vow those words; I actually vowed to "mutually honor and respect each other." And that vow had been crushed underfoot on that long-ago morning in the small trailer in my parent's orchard, soon after our honeymoon.

Once, a concerned friend talked to me about how Jason treated me, and I relayed the information back to Jason, glad that someone cared enough to notice. I wanted him to see that, if someone else had noticed, then it obviously must be true. I now know that a narcissist turns everything against their accuser; they can never be in the wrong.

"If they knew how hard it is to live with you, they would treat you the same way," he spat back at me with a hardened, angry face.

It was as if I had been slammed by a fist. Shocked and hurt, I believed him. I hated myself for being so awful. I decided to try harder to be a better person. But my many failings never seemed to go away or get better, even though I tried really hard. If I could just be what he wanted, I thought, maybe he would love me. Once I confided to Jason how hard it was to work on my imperfections and how I felt like a miserable failure.

"I'm glad I don't have any faults," he began. "If you think of yourself as a ship on a journey and steer toward the distant shore, you will eventually get there. It is easier to make small corrections along the way than to make a large correction all at once."

Thanking him for his advice, I believed him that he didn't have any faults and resolved to try to become like one of the saints I had read about as a girl. It must be my own failings that caused me to think I was neglected and unloved. He was the perfect husband, while I was a terrible wife. If I could just change, things would be better. It didn't matter how hard I tried, though... our relationship only got worse.

I was so discouraged. By that point, Jason's boundaries completely encompassed my own; I dared not step outside of them. He carefully controlled the fantasy world he had built around himself and did not like it when anyone shattered it. He had moved us a thousand miles away from my family, listened to my phone calls, read my correspondence, and insisted on approving my friends. The children and I were virtual prisoners in our own home and inside his fantasy world. Being a narcissist, he couldn't see anything wrong with controlling every aspect of our lives. It was *his world*. No one else could tell him otherwise. There were no longer two in our marriage; there was only one—Jason.

Tessy was gone.

If I could stand next to her right now, I would slap her in the face. "Wake up!"

I had forgotten that life had ever been different. I tried hard to please him in order to protect the children, so life didn't become any more of a living hell than it already was. I was afraid of what he would do if I stepped over the line. I didn't know what would happen, but it was implied.

Jason was a master at manipulating, twisting the truth, and instilling fear. He could lie so well that people would believe him, even if they had witnessed the truth. If he wanted to force you to believe something, he carefully and methodically twisted bits of information and implanted doubts until you were finally brainwashed. If you still resisted him, he would play emotional guilt games and use intimidation. He was extremely intelligent, and he used it, together with lying, to control those around him.

He did not like me crying, so I stopped whenever he was around. I tried hard to shove my feelings inside or turn them off. With his amazing talents, he never once made me a personal gift, although he made gifts for others. He didn't buy me birthday or Christmas presents either, but that wasn't a problem until the children were old enough to notice. I covered that over by buying myself a present and saying it was from him. On Christmas mornings, I always hoped my empty stocking would have something in it from him. It never did.

I realized in my heart that my life was just a series of lies as I covered for him and pretended we were a happy family. As the tension grew, I became more fearful and walked on eggshells every day.

NOW IT COMES TO RAPE

He wanted sex three times a day, so only getting it every night was already a suffering for him, he informed me.

THE ATMOSPHERE WAS HEAVY WITH RAGE. I worried about the loaded gun in the drawer of the nightstand next to Jason's side of the bed — it occurred to me that he might be thinking about killing me. The fact that I *expected* him to think like that, and that I accepted it as part of my life, was what was so abnormal. I was just a shell of the person I had once been, so it didn't occur to me that expecting one's husband to entertain thoughts of murder *isn't normal*. I pulled my heavy layers of blankets more tightly around my cowering body and faced the opposite direction. I was not permitted to get up and leave. No. That would never do.

As far as he was concerned, I was trying to force my will on him, and I was going to pay for it. He didn't want to have anything to do with Natural Family Planning (a Catholic-approved method of birth control accomplished by abstaining from sex), even with his ultra-Catholic beliefs that he laid on me and the children like a lead weight. But I was tired of having baby after baby without a break and with no help in sight; I was experiencing terrible exhaustion. He had begrudgingly gone along with my charting and abstaining during certain times of the month... for a while.

That night happened to be an "abstaining" night. According to the NFP, that meant no sex, if I wished to avoid another pregnancy.

Even during times when I had recently given birth or been up all night with a baby, his strict rule was that I was *never* allowed to say no to sex. He wanted sex three times a day, he had informed me, so only getting it once every night already made him suffer enough. That really left me no way out. As good Catholics, we were not allowed to use artificial birth control. The literature had promised that NFP would bring a couple closer together as they "cooperate in respecting each other's body." *Right, what a joke.* So, since it was an abstaining night, when I went to bed, I stayed as far away from him as I could and rolled over facing the wall. I thought it was the kind thing to do.

Earlier he had warned me, "I didn't get married to have to abstain."

His solution to birth control was, "You can have baby after baby until you almost die, and then the doctors will fix the problem, like they did to my mom and your mom." There was no concern for me or care about my physical or emotional wellbeing.

That night, he was seething; you could cut the air with a knife. I was afraid, thinking about the gun... Yet I was trying to stand up for myself and was desperate not to get pregnant again so soon. The room was freezing, as always, and the blankets were heaped in many suffocating layers. However, the coldest thing in the room wasn't the gun or the air—it was his heart.

With a sudden movement, he jumped up in the bed, flung back the blankets, and jerked my shoulder over so I lay on my back. Next, while yanking up my nightgown, he straddled me, forced my legs apart, and proceeded to rape me with such hatred that I could only feel shock. This was my husband, the person who I had hoped would love me the most in the world, and he was raping me with murderous rage. I trembled in fear and did nothing to stop him. I belonged to him, and he had every right to do whatever he wanted. At least I had been brainwashed to think that way.

"So it comes to rape," I whispered to the uncaring darkness as he dismounted, rolled over, and went to sleep.

I lay in the cold darkness like a person who had been shot. I had been right about the gun—he'd shot me. Not with a lead bullet, but a bullet of hate. He had blown a hole in my soul that changed me forever. I could never again have respect or love for such a monster.

Inside, I felt dead. A tidal wave of revulsion washed over me and threatened to drown me. Any feelings left for him were gone; I hated and despised this man who could treat a person the way he treated me. I was an object, a thing, a semen depository. I did not just hate him; I hated *myself* for allowing him to rape me and then doing nothing, absolutely nothing, about it. I loathed myself. Fear, overwhelming fear, paralyzed me. I was alone; there was no one to turn to. There was no way out.

If I could stand next to her now, I would hug her and whisper, "Run, run. It only gets worse…"

Because I did nothing, he despised me even more. Then I had to play the game that everything was okay and that it hadn't happened. Years later, he told me, "If I had known *you* thought it was rape, I wouldn't have done it."

That isn't an apology.

Somehow, life went on. I baked, cleaned, washed, nursed, sewed, cooked, taught and took care of my children. They were all that I had, and nothing else mattered anymore.

Depression weighed heavily on me. I was very sad and often

thought of death. Suicide, as an escape, eventually became my default mode of coping.

Falling Off My Pedestal

A few months later, Jason and a friend of his named Brian helped a neighbor with a remodel during the weekends. Brian started coming over to our house. He was a handsome man, gentle and kind. He spoke nicely and did thoughtful things for me. I found myself responding to this rare treatment, and my heart went out to him. Somehow, I no longer cared that it was wrong to think that way about someone who was not my husband. I desperately wanted out of the hell I existed in. I sent Brian a note and told him how I felt. He asked me what I wanted, and I replied that I did not want anything except to let someone know how horrible my life and marriage were. He responded that he also felt that Jason was critical and unkind, but that we would have to tell him about the note.

He didn't realize what really went on, or he might not have pursued this avenue. Being an upright man, Brian brought the note over and showed Jason.

I was fearful, yet a part of me no longer cared. Perhaps I even felt relief, hoping something would change.

So what if he killed me? He was probably going to anyway.

The blood drained from Jason's face when he read the note. He looked at me with cold eyes and asked me if I had written the note.

"Yes," I replied. "I am miserable in our marriage."

I thought he would go into a rage, but a funny thing happened. At first he accused me of "testing the waters," and then Jason said he would never speak to anyone about it and that it was over with. He ridiculed the idea that I was miserable or that Brian said he was critical. He told Brian that my brain was messed up because I had been in an accident when I was a teenager. Jason was more kindly toward me for a while afterward. He continued his friendship with Brian for many years, bringing him over to the house occasionally, to my great embarrassment but to Jason's deep satisfaction as he witnessed my shame.

Much later, it occurred to me that Jason may not have wanted anyone else to know about my transgression, at the time, because it made him look bad. He certainly didn't hold back later, when he did everything in his power to destroy me.

I took a dive off of my pedestal and never really climbed back up again. I hated myself—I had betrayed God and my marriage vows. I was a bad person, not the saint I had fantasized about. My ever-present interior sadness plunged me to an all-time low. My self-esteem and self-confidence plummeted even lower, if that was possible.

I needed to let someone know what was going on in my situation and get help. I longed to do something about it. Not only did I not have the courage, I didn't even know that something *could* be done about it. I believed that I would never be free. I had made a vow to God, and I intended to keep it no matter how hard things got. Even God couldn't get through that wall. I had the false pride that I would become a saint by allowing myself to be a doormat, by enduring terrible treatment (it's what I had read about in books about the saints).

Jason knew how I thought, and he reinforced it. My mother-in-law strongly supported that way of thinking, because it was how she conducted her own marriage; she was a "saintly martyr." My own parents were confused about what went on, but they had a "non-interference policy." I really couldn't blame anyone for my situation; I had stepped up on the martyr pedestal myself, but had finally fallen off of it—thank God. It would be years before God would be able to get through to me, but falling off my pedestal was the first crack in the foundation.

*　*　*

Jason insisted that the children needed to be spanked hard when punished. He said that my spankings were so soft, they did no good. The idea was to make sure the children knew you meant business. When Jason was growing up, he and his siblings were cruelly whipped and the punishments weren't balanced out by affection.

Their mother was a strict disciplinarian. In my childhood, we were spanked rarely; my parents felt other deterrents should be used first.

I wasn't convinced Jason was right but tried to do what he wanted. He showed me in the Bible where parents were admonished to discipline their children. So God was on his side. We used wooden spoons or a paddle for spanking. A few times, the spoon broke when I spanked—I was getting more proficient. Then one day Jason spanked Aleena with such a severe blow of the wooden paddle that she screamed with a high-pitched, horrifying wail that cut through me like a knife. When he left, I checked her behind. A large, horrible, raised red welt had appeared on the back of her upper thigh; it looked like the skin had almost split and a bruise was already forming. I was angry and told him he had hit her too hard, but he denied it was wrong and insisted that she had needed the punishment. Actually, she hadn't done anything wrong; Jason had punished all of the children because the guilty party had not come forward when he asked who had committed some offense. I tried to avoid spankings after that. Instead, I used restrictions and encouragements more often. I felt bad about the spankings and resolved only to use spankings for defiance or danger.

Jason did not like that I no longer gave myself fully to him as I had when we were first married. I stopped being passionate, loving, and open-hearted; instead, I became distant and reserved. How could a woman feel loved by a man who had raped her? When I tried to tell him I did not feel loved and that I needed to feel loved to respond with love, it angered him.

With bitterness, he demanded, "What do I have to do to prove it?"

When a man has to ask that question in such a negative tone, proof no longer matters. As the marriage deteriorated, I would no longer kiss him on the lips. His habit of chewing tobacco and spitting the juice into beer bottles left around the house, or filling a dirty spittoon and never brushing his teeth, made kissing him repellant. It would have been a token kiss anyway.

There was no passion or love left.

1989: MOVING TO COOPERTON, IDAHO

If you've never been in 30°F below zero weather, the fierce cold clutches like an iron claw. You have to cover your nose to warm the air before breathing it in, because air that cold feels like needles stabbing your nose, throat, and lungs. You have to keep your eyes almost shut to keep the tears covering your eyes from freezing.

JASON COULDN'T FIND A DECENT JOB IN THE AREA. He bucked hay a few times, which was very hard labor. He worked for the butcher at the store, but the knife slipped, and he almost couldn't have any more children, an incident that amused the ladies who worked in the store. He helped with a remodel and almost blinded himself in one eye after an accident with a screwdriver.

Then, Jason's younger brother Joshua sent him a new computer. Jason had learned to program with a home computer called a TRS-80 when it first came out. We still lived in the "Mouse House" then. He also had a Commodore 64 and a 128 computer. The newer computer came with CRT monitor and was loaded with the cutting-edge (at the time) Windows 3.0. He began to study all day, every day, to be an engineer. No degree, no schooling, but a self-made engineer, nonetheless. He decided to open an engineering firm, and he called it Alliant Engineering. He didn't have a business license, and there were no funds to start a new venture. I was tired of supporting his dreams and asked him to find a real job; I didn't see how he could start his own business on less than $2,000 per year. We needed to pay the mortgage and bills. The kids needed clothes and food. Jason was angry and upset that I was not more supportive, but he started looking for work.

He finally found a job in Canton, Idaho, four hours' drive north, as VP of engineering for a startup company. Jason and the owner were the only ones working for the business. He began commuting. Since we couldn't find rentals that would accept large families, it was the beginning of decades of commuting long distances and coming home on weekends, first at this new job, which lasted two years, and then at his subsequent jobs. I would pack him enough food to last the work week. He usually lived in his office, slept on the floor, and didn't shower until he got home on the weekends. Sometimes, one of his co-workers took pity—or wanted a reprieve from the smell—and invited him to their home for a shower and dinner. After work in the evenings, for relaxation, he would have what he called "beer thirty" with a few of the other workers who wanted to join in. Jason liked his solitude, and I believe he liked being away from his ever-growing brood. He never wanted to work a nine-to-five job, so I was continually amazed and appreciative that he did so.

Besides being pregnant with my fifth child, I took on homeschooling the children. Homeschooling began as a talk between us. It was a new thing, this homeschooling, and I wasn't sure I could do it. There was a story in the news about a woman who had been jailed for homeschooling her children and then had died in jail; Idaho subsequently passed a law dropping most restrictions for homeschooling.

My two oldest children were in the first part of their second year in public school when Jason decided that I could try homeschooling. We used a Catholic correspondence school that sent poorly-copied, out-of-date (pre-Vatican II) books and materials, and so I taught. It was overwhelming for me and too expensive for us. We passed the same books and materials down to the next child and saved on expenses that way. At the time, we believed that we would be protecting our children from the bad influence of social morality. I didn't realize that I was helping to set up a situation where our family was even more socially isolated. Later, our children would be at a great disadvantage when they did not possess the interpersonal skills to get jobs or form relationships, due to their social awkwardness.

The kids seemed happy to be at home with mom, especially

when it was thirty below zero outside. No one wanted to crawl out of bed in the morning, since it was also below-freezing in the house, to go off to school.

If you've never been in 30°F-below-zero weather, the fierce cold clutches like an iron claw. You have to cover your nose to warm the air before breathing it in, because air that cold feels like needles stabbing your nose, throat, and lungs. Your eyes must be almost shut to prevent the tears covering your eyes from freezing. I had to be careful about going outside when it was that cold. I didn't know it then, but I had a thyroid condition, which made it difficult for me to keep warm. My core temperature was a few degrees lower than the average person's. I suffered so much from being cold that I have a great dread of it even now.

During this time, while Jason did the four-hour commute to his job and only came home on weekends, I felt alone but relieved. I couldn't drive, was housebound, and had four small children to care for with one on the way. On the weekends, when he came home, we did our major grocery shopping in one of the larger towns. Sometimes we made a whole day of it and drove over the border to Oregon to do bulk shopping, doctor visits, and errands. Other times, we went to church in a nearby town and then shopped afterward. The small convenience stores in Aldridge had higher prices, and it was challenging to stretch our food dollars unless we shopped farther away.

* * *

In the summer of 1989, I was worn out, carrying my fifth child. After enduring rape, I knew that Jason would not agree to space out the birth of children, nor would he help with homeschooling, the yard, garden work, or housework. I couldn't escape the terrible hopelessness I often felt between the continual childbearing, social isolation, and feeling imprisoned in my own home. I kept up the façade that we were a good, holy Catholic family and sometimes even believed it. But I knew the marriage was rotten at its core. I had betrayed God, and Jason wasn't capable of love or empathy.

My body changed after having my third child. Labor became more difficult, and this one proved to be my hardest. I labored for three days off and on. Since contractions began over the weekend, Jason didn't make the commute to work; he was able to drive me the two hours to see my obstetrician. I was over three centimeters dilated, and the doctor would not let me make the long trip back home on the winding mountain roads. He decided to break the membranes. Suddenly, after three days of moderate-paced labor, I began experiencing very hard contractions. My blood sugar also plunged, causing shaking and weakness.

I lost control, as the contractions came on like a freight train. They continued to ramp up until there were almost no valleys, only peaks, one building right on top of the other. I was sure I would die. With such intense pain and pressure, I began to "check out" at the height of each contraction. I called on God to help me. From that moment, instead of feeling like I would die as the contraction reached its peak, I felt a surge of great joy. Somewhere I had heard that pain and pleasure were divided by a razor-thin line. That day, it was true.

When my baby girl was born, the infant surprised everyone in the room by saying quite clearly, "Mama."

Her father held the sweet bundle on his chest, glanced down at her, and said, "No way." He was amazed that something that size had been tucked inside my body. How did she ever get out? She was only a moderately large baby, but for some reason it occurred to him for the first time how difficult labor and birth must be for a woman. He allowed me to name our baby that time. I think he felt I deserved a prize after suffering such a long, hard labor. It was the only time I named one of the children. I named her Angela, after a movie star. Aleena was ecstatic to finally have a sister. She had been surrounded by brothers, and now she had her very own sister.

Eventually, Jason found a rental house in Cooperton, a town near his job, large enough to fit our growing brood. It was rare to find someone who would permit us to rent from them with our large family. Legally, a landlord can't deny you on the basis of familial status, but they always did. Once they heard you had five children, for one reason or another, the rental was no longer available.

When baby Angela was a few months old, we were able to make the move to Cooperton, Idaho. The house was a twenty-minute commute from Jason's work and a four-hour drive from our Idaho home.

The rental house was a drafty, two-story, older Victorian home but in much better condition than the Aldridge house. It had new carpeting, wild, mismatched wallpaper, and several bathrooms. The house sat in a tiny town surrounded by wheat fields. I could walk around the small town and visit church once in a while with my babies in tow. There were a few small shops in town, but most people went south to do grocery shopping in Derrington or north to Canton-Fuller. Fuller was across the border in Washington.

* * *

There was a cat killer in the town who lived right across the street from us. He trapped wandering cats, and the poor felines were never seen again. I was suspicious after he stopped by and asked if the feral kittens on the side of our house were mine. I replied, "No, they seem to be wild cats." The kittens disappeared the next day and were never seen again.

That year, the Berlin Wall came down, a long-running miniseries about the Civil War was watched by horrified viewers across the nation, and… my baby Angela woke up every hour on the hour for eighteen months straight. The scary cat-killer neighbor walked into our home through the back door without knocking one day and gave me a shock. I locked the doors after that.

I seemed to be going through some sort of spiritual darkness, so sometimes, on our walk, the children and I would visit the church. We sat in a pew nearest the tabernacle. Convinced that I was a terrible person, I felt selfish for not wanting to homeschool or have any more babies. Exhaustion and numbness were my main feelings, while thoughts of suicide were ever-present.

* * *

The children enjoyed the large, drafty house. It had plenty of places

to hide and play. My sweet baby Angela soon grew old enough—just barely—to dance around the house. She was so little that seeing her dance caused the neighbors to smile. This little daughter of mine did *not* smile, though. Her baby face bore a grim expression as she danced. Angela spent most of her time clinging to my skirts and wouldn't even allow me go to the bathroom alone. She still woke up every hour all night long for eighteen months straight.

The job in Canton, Idaho, didn't last very long. After working there almost two years, Jason lost his job, so we packed up the children and moved back to our Idaho home in the mountains. Neglected, it was still there waiting for us.

CHAPTER 3:
DECADE 2, YEAR 1990

RETURN TO ALDRIDGE

*At one time, fall was my favorite season, but not anymore.
Now it signaled that winter and terrible suffering were
ahead. I came to dread winter and hate the cold. I found
no joy in the snow and cold, which kept us locked inside
for months at a time and froze the hands and feet of my
children inside their own home.*

THE OLD ALDRIDGE HOUSE WAS STILL FILLED with our junk when we
arrived back home. We had not rented it out because it was in such
poor condition—no one would have wanted to live in it. So we left
it unattended and unheated while we were away. The floors were
still splintered, the walls were falling apart in chunks, and the paint
peeled in many places. The water heater had flooded the washroom;
the floor buckled up and re-dried in that warped fashion. It was
hard to walk on.

In the kitchen, the ceiling drywall sagged worse than before; the
huge gaping hole continued to dump dirt and debris onto the

kitchen table. Years before, when the eldest children were still babies, I repainted the kitchen cabinets and covered the walls in cheap plastic peel-and-stick wallpaper which I had picked up at a yard sale but there were holes in the once white linoleum near the sink and the range. The floor was so worn it was impossible to keep clean.

I could no longer put up with the kitchen ceiling. I knew how long it would take if I asked Jason for help, so one day, when he was out, I tore the sheetrock down. I was surprised to see vintage tongue-and-groove ceiling boards underneath which looked much better than the decayed drywall; they also went along with the style of the house. Water damage from the leaky roof had caused the dry wall decay. By peering through some of the cracks in the ceiling boards, I could see the sky in many places through the roof.

The ceiling boards needed a coat of paint, which we couldn't afford. I rounded up the paint we did have and mixed them together then tried to filter out the paint chunks that had partly dried inside the cans. When I was done, there was enough cream-colored paint to cover the ceiling. It didn't look too bad—I was happy with it. And Jason had a strange look on his face when he saw what I had accomplished.

Next, I decided to rip up the dirty linoleum. It had been a pain for years, showing every piece of dirt, and had to be mopped every day to look even halfway decent. The floor sloped downward toward the back of the kitchen due to the lack of a foundation. As we tore off the top layer of linoleum, we saw that it had been laid over layers of previously installed flooring. It was fun to see the bizarre colors and old tile patterns of years gone by. I was happy to uncover more tongue-and-groove boards once we reached the bottom layer.

* * *

The years passed and the children grew, not only in height but also in number. The boys slept upstairs, cut off from the heat since the stairway door was kept closed. Paint peeled in layers from the walls revealing a motley pattern of colors, and flakes littered their beds, the floor, and the stairs. The rotted plaster that clung desperately to

the ceiling lath overhead began to let go in chunks, randomly falling to the floor below. Jason stuffed roll-out insulation into the gaping holes to keep the heat from escaping through the roof. The upstairs floor was heated by the downstairs stove, which provided some warmth. The house received blown-in insulation the year after we qualified for energy assistance. It helped some but just wasn't enough.

There was still a great deal of decay in the ancient house, but, little by little, things were looking better. The house remained cold and drafty in the winter—it never would be cozy and warm. Winter in the mountains could, and usually did, last nine months, and then suddenly, almost without warning, summer would arrive. The in-between seasons of fall and spring were more like an intermission break. At one time, fall was my favorite season but it became a signal that winter, with its inescapable suffering, loomed ahead.

The younger children slept on mattresses laid on the floor in the dining room. The girls shared an older wood-frame bed and had their own room that we painted pink. I sewed them doll clothes to made a miniature quilt stamps. I saved a small, hand-knitted pink sweater that I had made for Aleena when she was a baby, with a pattern of white hearts across the chest and miniature rose buttons. Angela wore it next. Long after that, the little pink sweater was worn by my third daughter, my last child. Then it went with Aleena when she got married and, after many years, would be passed down to *her* first daughter, my granddaughter…

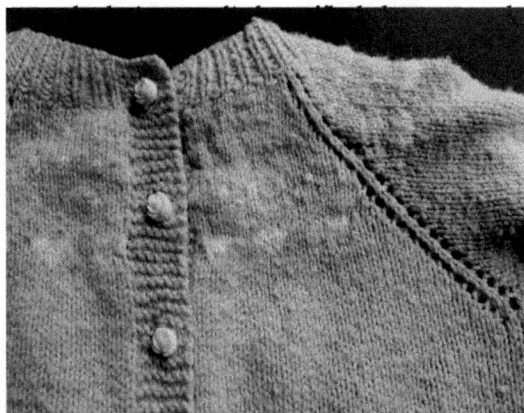

But we are getting ahead of ourselves here!

The room upstairs was divided by the stairs, and one boy slept on either side. There were two dormers on the south side of the house. All of our windows were outdated sash windows, the kind that can let go abruptly and plummet with a loud crash. They were drafty where the wood had shrunk, which also caused them to rattle and most had no screens. Once, a bat flew through an open window and hugged its soft body against the dining room wall. When Jason tried to kill it with a broom handle, it turned its little head around and screamed at him with demonic rage. There was a bat bloodstain on the unpainted plaster wall for years, a fitting baptism.

Right at the top of the stairs, in the ceiling, was a large hole of decayed, broken plaster where rotted, water-stained lath showed through. Any heat going up the stairwell raced up and out of the hole and then through the leaky roof. There were "hidey holes" to

play in under the eaves inside, where the builder had closed in a space on either side of the house. They were big enough to crawl into and store boxes but were a bit scary, too, because some of the spaces went down through the floor along the wall and then all the way to the bottom of the house. If you dropped anything down one of those spaces, you would never get it back. Thank goodness they were too small to accommodate a child.

One more room at the head of the stairs led to the outside, screen-enclosed porch that I described earlier as being the children's favorite summer sleeping place. Ryan, our eldest, stayed in that room next to the porch. It was far away from the downstairs heat and the door leading to the outside porch was very drafty, so his room was very uncomfortable regardless of the season.

After a year of searching, Jason was offered a new job at a business called Aquatronics, Inc., situated in a Washington border town called Fuller. It was right across the border from his earlier job in Canton, Idaho.

So, he began to commute again. He would leave early Monday morning in time to get to work by 9:00 a.m., as the commute was four hours. He then worked long days in order to come home Thursday evenings and once again slept in his office on the floor, unable to bathe. That was when he began using deodorant, and I resumed packing a box of food to last him through four-day workweeks.

*   *   *

As winter asserted itself once again, the woodstove had to be fed continually in an attempt to keep the house warm. Kindling needed to be split if it ran out, and since I couldn't take a stroller out in the snow, I ventured out with one or two of the children for groceries or to check the mail. Mostly, however, I was stuck indoors much of the winter with homeschooling, babies, and chores. My very favorite thing to do was to take a hot bath—it was the only way to get warm.

The children enjoyed playing out in the snow. They built snow forts and sledded but did not have adequate clothing; their hand-knitted mittens were not made of wool and didn't keep their hands very warm. I tried to get the new, thick, warm gloves whenever I could. And sometimes, they wore several pair of socks over their hands, which helped, until they got wet.

Brent was so cold one morning that he got too close to the woodstove and burned his back. On another evening, I struggled to cram a really large, heavy log into the stove, hoping it would burn all night with the damper turned low. But the log got firmly stuck halfway into the stove opening and then caught on fire with half the log still hanging out. I stared in horror as the flames engulfed it and didn't know what to do, so I called the fire chief who lived right down the road. He arrived quickly. By then, the draft around the log made a roaring sound. He grabbed the part of the log that still hung outside the woodstove and, with a strong tug, pulled it out, ran out the front door with the burning log in his hands, and placed it on the cement walk where he then doused it with snow. I never again tried to cram a large log into the woodstove!

It was a challenge every morning to leave my warm cocoon of blankets as dawn was breaking, step onto a freezing floor, and start a fire or fan the few remaining coals into flame in order to warm the house. Once the fire was crackling, though, I would make a pan of hot cereal and toast home-baked bread to warm everyone up as they started their day. We ate, did our morning chores and then worked on homeschooling. Sometimes we enjoyed crafts or science projects. The kids were all very creative and artistic. They carved soap sculptures, played with their soft dolls or Barbies, made forts, and put together puzzles or played with cards. We had our nap time each afternoon where we all lay down and read books or slept. That gave me some time to rest with the baby of the moment.

* * *

I was pregnant again, for the sixth time. After the terrible labor with my last pregnancy, I lived in dread of labor and birth. I gave up hoping that Jason would ever follow some sort of child-spacing or family-planning method. He simply didn't care about me. Although my children gave me great joy, I did not want to bear a baby every two years until menopause.

As a believing Catholic, I did not have the choice of using birth control, except for Natural Family Planning—which isn't an option unless you have a cooperative partner. Besides, it had resulted in my being raped earlier in the marriage. Since I would not abandon my babies or kill anyone, there seemed to be only one avenue left… and that was to accept my lot in life. I was in a bad marriage, and I had to live with it. It never occurred to me that I was living with abuse and should get help. Was any help available? I had no idea. Where could I have gone with five children, pregnant, and with no way to leave but walk?

I was imprisoned by fear and lack of self-esteem, and by having been brainwashed into believing that I didn't have the right to make my own choices. I could have called the sheriff for help to get away; I could have taken the kids and just started walking; I could have called a family member a thousand miles away, and likely someone would have helped us. But it didn't occur to me, because I didn't believe I had the right to leave.

In desperation, I secretly visited the doctor when he came to our small clinic in town, and I asked for help with my deep depression.

He put me on an anti-depressant.

Jason became enraged when he found out I was taking something without his permission. "It's a mind-altering drug, and the effect it could have on *my* marriage is unimaginable," he screamed at me.

I was prepared to answer him. "Perhaps it will make me happier, and I will enjoy sex more." I was learning to play his game.

He ceded at that point.

Taking an anti-depressant did not make me happier. It deadened my emotions—which actually brought some relief, but not happiness—and did not do anything for desire; quite the opposite, actually.

*   *   *

In earlier pregnancies, I suffered from extreme heartburn. The doctor said that acid reflux had scarred my esophagus. Years earlier, after my fourth child Brent was born, my doctor told me not to have any more babies. It was his opinion that, with the continuing damage to my esophagus, I would end up living with a feeding tube. It was my sixth pregnancy and clear that this would be my largest baby. As the pregnancy neared completion, I needed lots of pillows to prop me up so I could sleep. I had three under my shoulders and head, one or two between my knees, and several tucked under my back, to keep me on my side—there was *no way* I could lie on my back. I had trouble breathing, and, finally, one of my ribs dislocated. My tailbone had been dislocated during my first pregnancy, and with every subsequent pregnancy it gave me trouble. In the last few weeks, I was only able to eat vanilla ice cream; nothing else would keep the terrible acid reflux at bay.

Labor started in the wee hours of the morning, and the baby dropped low very quickly. Jason wanted to stay and make a pot of coffee before we left on our two-hour drive to the birthing center in Shandon, Idaho. He thought this one would take days, like the other labors had. He was wrong. I insisted that he take me immediately and forget the coffee, which surprised him, and he complied. Fifteen minutes after we arrived at the birthing center, my largest baby, Joseph, made his arrival. He weighed just a few ounces under ten pounds. I was amazed that such a large baby could be birthed so quickly and, compared to the other labors, so easily. Joseph was an amazingly strong, healthy, happy baby. He didn't seem to be plagued with the stomach sensitivity problems and colic that most of my others had suffered.

Jason still commuted, all the while keeping an eye out for a rental. As usual, a rental house was hard to find for a large family. But I was happy when he commuted. It gave me some time away from him and the dread that arose when he was around since I never knew when he might get upset over some small thing. I always tried to detect when he would get angry and attempted to deflect it somehow. He would sulk or give me the silent treatment whenever he wanted to control or punish me for not doing his will. He told me that, if a marriage ever broke up, it was always the woman's fault, because the man was not getting enough sex. His mother once stated that marital problems were usually the woman's fault.

Early in our relationship, Jason hammered it in that Catholics should never even consider divorce. I felt strange every time he mentioned it, almost as a warning. I went along with him on the outside, but inside, I wished it wasn't so. Marriage is a sacrament in the Catholic Church, and I strongly believe the church is right to defend sacramental marriage. But having a partner who wouldn't cooperate with spacing pregnancies or help with childrearing and who treated me with such contempt was tearing the very fabric of my soul to pieces. It felt like I had been imprisoned for life without parole. I was in a terrible state of continual anguish.

I went from feeling that God is a loving Father to wondering if He really is a terrible God, keeping some large score book of punishments and damnation, like my husband seemed to think. Did God care more about rules and regulations than love, I wondered. I felt that the loving God I had once known from my childhood had abandoned me. After much thought, I decided the situation must be my fault and became determined to be a better wife and mother and to follow God no matter how hard it became. Instead of escaping my prison, I turned the key and locked myself in. I didn't know that the church doesn't expect anyone to stay in an abusive relationship. I thought "for better or for worse" meant no matter how bad it got. I was wrong, and it continued to get worse.

I blamed myself, and, instead of drawing boundaries and having strength, I retreated, scared, and took the easy way out, which was the hardest way of all. What a coward I was; I understand that now, especially when I look back and see that it was the children who suffered due to my lack of courage. I was so wrapped up in my own suffering that I didn't see just how much they suffered or what a bad example a loveless, terrible marriage was for them. My greatest shame is that I let them down; I lived with my head in the sand, unaware of what was really going on.

RESPITE – MARCEL

They screamed down the hill on the plastic sled, only to realize at the last moment that there was a barbed wire fence at the bottom. Their mother watched them from the house porch with her heart in her mouth.

JASON WAS BRILLIANT. He invented a laser device used in agriculture. His idea was patented, and because of that, he landed the job at Aquatronics, Inc. He became their senior engineer, even though he only had an eighth-grade education. He was quite a genius in many ways. When he invented, he thought out the product from start to finish as it went through the manufacturing process. He could do anything in a machine shop. He didn't like people, though, and his antisocial qualities hindered his career.

He continued the four-hour commute from Aldridge, Idaho, while I stayed home with the children. In his spare time, he played his banjo endlessly and sometimes, his fiddle. He was proud of his brood but he couldn't figure out why his marriage was in shambles. His threshold for deprivation, suffering, and pain was so high that he didn't even notice when other people suffered. He had learned to shut off the world around him long before, as a child, and had carried that into adulthood.

Jason's new boss tried to talk him into purchasing a house locally; there was a nice one in the Fuller area for $80,000. But Jason had repeatedly told me over the years, "I will not buy someone else's crap. Someday, I will build you a house."

He finally found a large two-story farmhouse to rent; it was outside of Marcel, Washington, surrounded by wheat fields. Planes overhead and farmers on their tractors both sprayed chemicals all around us, just like in Cooperton. The difference was, because ours was the only house in the midst of many acres, they liberally sprayed directly overhead.

*   *   *

My seventh baby was born several months after we moved to the Marcel house—a sweet, gentle baby boy we named Benjamin. He announced his imminent arrival by breaking the bag of water while I lay in bed. Jason's parents arrived soon after, to help out. They had moved up to the Aldridge area a few years before, four hours' drive away. The children were so well trained to help around the house that grandma felt unneeded. But when I came home from the hospital to a freshly made, turned-down bed, I was grateful.

In late spring, I planted a garden. I had always loved gardening. It felt wonderful to be in a real home that was warm and comfortable.

However, I still didn't drive. The house was out in the country, where it was too far to walk to town, and we had no neighbors. We were pretty isolated.

All of the hills surrounding the farmhouse were planted with wheat or chickpeas, the main crops of eastern Washington. After harvest, the shorn golden wheat fields were a great temptation for the children: the hills were very slippery with the thick cover of dry stubble. After one harvest, my oldest son, Ryan, tried to ski on the shimmery stubble with outdated bind-on skis. When he fell, the skis did not release, but his knee did. He tore his ligament and permanently damaged the joint. Jason never could empathize with another person's pain. He was certain that Ryan was exaggerating, until the knee became very swollen; a trip to the doctor confirmed his stretched and torn ligament. Ryan never fully recovered from the injury. I remember seeing my young teenage son crawling on his knees up the hill to the house after his father refused to assist him.

The two girls went sledding on the shorn fields. They screamed down the hill on the plastic sled, only to realize at the last moment that there was a barbed wire fence at the bottom. I watched them from the house porch with my heart in my mouth, figuring they were going to become lunchmeat as I was helpless to do anything to stop it. At the last moment, they realized the danger and lay really low on the sled, miraculously slipping below the bottom wire and escaping without injury. It's amazing that children live through childhood.

During the winter, the basement was turned into a learning space for the boys, as they watched their dad show them, for the first time, how to do woodworking and carving. Finally, they were learning skills from their very talented father, as he whittled small rabbits for his daughters and worked on carving a face for a violin he was handcrafting. A little chair was turned on a lathe, crafted by Alex for his solemn little sister as a Christmas present. I was happy that Jason was finally passing on these skills to his sons.

Jason spent most of his free time playing bluegrass songs on his banjo or violin. He had a secret hope that he would be one of the great banjo talents in the music world. I think that music must have made sense to him in a senseless world. As his children got older, he spent more time with them, too. He was very strict, but there was pride in his eyes as his sons mastered skills and revealed that they were also quite talented, as well.

Ryan used one of the large closets as his bedroom and created a finely-detailed set of aircraft out of cardboard to while away the hours. I regretted that he hid the airplanes under a space in the floorboards and didn't keep them. He had discovered that the floorboards in his closet space had a secret opening and was elated to find antique treasures hidden underneath, hidden most likely by a child, decades earlier. There was an old clock, tools, and other assorted items. Ryan put everything back carefully and added his airplanes to the collection. When he was a very small boy, he carefully crafted detailed cardboard items and wondered why his replicas of a 3.5-inch floppy or small camera made in the exact size and shape of originals wouldn't work the same way. When computers became available to the home user, he dove in and never came up; he not only taught himself to program but taught his younger brothers, as well.

Aleena, just entering her teen years, enjoyed trying her hand at cooking and was a natural. One morning, while she griddled up some pancakes, she felt a ferocious sneeze come on. Instead of turning her head to sneeze, she covered her nose and mouth tightly and blew it into her ears. Poor sweetheart: she was just trying to avoid contaminating everyone's food, but she ruined her ears. Her ears not only were damaged; they continued to get repeated infections, including fungus growing in the ear canal. She made great pancakes, though. I told her that sneezing on the pancakes would have been better than blowing out her ear drums: you can always toss the pancakes in the trash and start over.

Jason decided to take Tae Kwon Do, and he brought the three oldest boys along with him so they could learn, as well. The boys enjoyed going to class and learning the discipline and moves. But one day, they brought home something other than their excitement. Another student in the class had come down with chicken pox, which my sons brought back home to their siblings. Being isolated, none of my children had ever had chicken pox and they were miserable. The older the child, the worse the symptoms were. Being a young teen, Ryan fared the worst. He had chicken pox inside his eyeballs and got so sick, the doctor thought he was losing his sight. Baby Benjamin only got a few of the pox and barely ran a temperature. It was a challenge to have a whole house full of very sick kids. Marlene, a woman from church, brought some food by for us, as well as soothing oatmeal-bath packets for the children. I was very sorry for them but also glad that they wouldn't have to suffer with the virus as adults.

*　*　*

My younger daughter, Angela—the child who danced with a grim face as a baby—was a spitfire. She earned the honor of being a "woman driver" before she was even seven. Angela crawled into a large wheeled cart used around the farm that had a metal tongue. It was on an incline, so it began to roll. She never made a peep as it went barreling into one of the cars and put a large dent in it. Try explaining to the insurance company how your six-year-old daughter wrecked the car!

In that area around Marcel, the soil is some of the most over-cropped soil in the northwestern United States. It is a fine talcum-powder soil. When the farmers till it, large dust clouds are launched in the air and spread throughout the surrounding area. The residents have lung problems and a high cancer rate from the dust mixed with the chemical cocktail that is heavily sprayed on the crops every year. When it rains, the soil turns into slick snot, and a car's tires will spin like it's on ice. We got stuck on a back road once when a heavy thunderhead let loose quite suddenly. We began to slide off the road into a ditch. Jason gunned the engine, spun the wheels, and, by sheer momentum, escaped to a nearby paved road, spitting mud in all direction.

We traveled the back roads often on his days off in a kind of desperation, trying to find a house for sale that was tucked away in the fields. He was searching for a broken-down fixer-upper, so he could get a good deal and then put sweat equity into it. I still hoped that, one day, we would fix up or build a home of our own. I didn't realize that he would never fix up any place... unless he was going to sell it. I longed for a decent home.

The Marcel rental was expensive, and ultimately an incident occurred there that propelled us to move as soon as we could.

One day, the kitchen cabinets filled with all of our chinaware, glasses, and bowls suddenly detached from the wall and crashed down onto my sister and her baby, who happened to be visiting at the time. Brent jumped in front of his aunt and baby cousin, shielding them from raining dishes, and was hurt in the process.

The sound was deafening. Broken shards of glass and dishware covered the kitchen floor. It was discovered that only two screws had held up the entire large set of cabinets. The landlord was in a nearby field and came in to see what the commotion was all about. He fixed the cupboard but blamed *us* for the incident, saying that we had put too much weight in the cupboards. We felt insulted to be blamed, when it was obvious that two small screws were terribly inadequate to hold up the loaded weight of kitchen cabinets.

Another time, the owners stopped by, got down on their hands and knees, and began to comb through the deep burnt-orange shag with their fingers, inspecting how clean the carpet was being kept. I was embarrassed for them, and couldn't believe my eyes.

Jason continued to look for a house to buy.

One weekend, we played kickball outside in one of the farm fields with our adopted Uncle Bill. He could kick the ball a long way, and it went up behind an old decrepit trailer that was falling apart and overrun with mice. The roof was full of holes, causing the ceiling tiles to crumble and scatter all over the floor. While retrieving the ball, I looked in the dirty windows and was glad that I didn't have to live there. It was a good thing I couldn't see into the future. Uncle Bill was a kind man and a good friend of the family; he was also an engineer and worked at the same company as Jason did. He encouraged our oldest son to enter a robot competition and helped our family in many ways.

Mice were a problem in the whole surrounding area. With the

large fields and outbuildings, the little critters were everywhere. One day, Jason discovered that they had nested in the back of his commuter car, and he wanted it cleaned out. Hanta virus was fresh news in those days, as was the fear of contracting it. I offered to clean it out, but Jason wouldn't have it—he demanded that one of the boys do the job.

He chose our second son, Alex, saying, "I have to support the family, and you are my wife. We can't take the risk. He can do it." I was shocked and appalled beyond measure, and I wanted to fight him about it, but Jason was adamant and would not put up with me back-talking him.

I had Alex cover his nose with a wet rag and use gloves. Nothing happened, and my worry was unfounded, but the incident made me furious. *Why couldn't I stand up to him? Why?*

* * *

After two years of living in the comfortable farmhouse, Jason found seventy-six acres of land in Remington, Idaho, about an hour's drive to the east, across the Washington border in Idaho. The land had been clear-cut years before and planted in barley. There were still slash piles of rotting logs scattered throughout the acreage, which were partially covered in dirt, grass, and moss. Nine of the seventy-six acres, in the remote corner of the property, were heavily treed, and one of the sides abutted a county road. The property was made up of steeply rolling hills with deep valleys and a few high plateau areas that were somewhat flat. Jason took us to see the property. He was excited about it. The land cost as much as a nice home, but there was no home on it. He told us it would be a sacrifice, and we would have to suffer for three years, but during that time, he would build us a home.

I struggled to climb up the first steep hill and didn't see how it was possible to live up there. I didn't want to do it. I knew it would be hard, but Jason always wanted to live off the land in a remote place, removed from society. Remember, when I married him, he was living the life of a mountain man.

It took about an hour to drive to the nearest populated area from the property, so we would be very isolated. There was no phone service, no electricity, no water—nothing but stubbled barley fields, a few trees in the ravines, and the nine acres of trees in the corner of the parcel. However, our piece of land was totally surrounded by forests, and a few neighbors were scattered around the lower areas. It was a very beautiful place.

Jason said it was our decision… but we would finally have a house, if we pulled together. As he knew it would, talk of a house made hope flare up in my heart once again (holding out a house as a carrot was the trump card, he used for controlling me). I talked to the kids while Jason was at work, and together we decided to support him in his dream. Wasn't a good wife supportive? I still figured that, if I just sacrificed more and was a better wife, our marriage would get better.

1995: THREE YEARS OF HELL— REMINGTON, IDAHO

"With the sun overhead, I lay down between the stubbled rows of barley. My pregnant body was tired, and there was nowhere else to lie. I watched as the well-drillers sank a twisting bit into the soil far below me in the fold of the two hills. Skimpy clouds danced in front of the sun. My fingers reached out to caress the powder-soft dirt. It had not rained for some time. In that moment, I found peace, even while the doomed child in my womb grew… and as my other children played on the seventy-six acres, which were to become our hell."

—Tessy's writings

JASON LOOKED INTO DRILLING A WELL ON THE LAND. The exuberant real estate agent asked me if this was to be my dream home. My heart sank; it was not my dream to be so isolated—it was his.

My heartbeat became irregular; I felt like it was pushing up into my throat. It would catch there, fluttering, and make me choke. Jason took me to the doctor, and I was put on a monitor. I definitely had a skip.

My husband told the doctor it was nothing. "She's upset because soon she won't have any place to live. She is just under a lot of stress," Jason declared, as he made the diagnosis for the doctor.

The doctor gave him a strange look but did not ask any questions.

The stress *was* terrible. I was getting rid of unnecessary items, packing boxes, and cleaning the house so we could move to a barren mountaintop covered in slash piles and barley stubble.

About that time, I had a vivid spiritual experience which I kept secret. It happened one night while the rest of the family was sleeping. As I was praying, I was suddenly caught up in spirit and felt like a speck in the vast expanse of eternity. Then a presence asked me for one of my children. It was so real. I was overwhelmed and started crying. I pondered the question, convinced it was God who was asking.

Finally I made a deal. "You can have one of my children," I said, "if you take the child to heaven with you." I figured, if it really was God, how could I refuse?

The presence withdrew. I didn't know what had happened, but I thought about it often, and then I finally wondered if it was just my imagination. A few weeks later, I found out I was pregnant with my eighth child.

CHAPTER 4:
FIRST YEAR ON THE MOUNTAIN

The jonny cakes browned on one side then I flipped them to crisp on the other side. Eggs sizzled in the butter, and then I served the jonny cakes with an egg perched on top and butter dripping down the sides. The over-easy eggs broke open as they ate them, the yellow, eggy goodness covering everything like syrup on pancakes. The children formed a ring around me as I cooked and hungrily took their turns as the steaming feast came off the griddle. It was so wonderful to eat a hot meal that they couldn't get enough, especially after weeks of cold, starchy food.

— Tessy's writings

BEFORE WE MOVED FROM MARCEL, Jason scouted around for a trailer for us to live in. He approached the owners of the Marcel rental and inquired about the derelict thirty-two foot trailer sitting outside the house, the same one I had peered into the day we'd played ball with Uncle Bill. The owners gladly gave him the trailer; it was too expensive for them to haul it to the dump. However, they stipulated that the trailer could not be worked on or cleaned while it was still on their property. That made it very difficult for us, because there was no electricity or water where we were going.

Jason asked his boss, Darrel, for help hauling the trailer to the seventy-six acres with his three-quarter-ton truck. Darrel lived near Remington and was a very nice man. He allowed our family to heap a mountain of boxes and stuff in his garage until our new house was built; poor guy—if he'd only known. After leaving the country road, his truck had a hard time hauling the trailer up the first steep hill, but thankfully it was still dry, and he accomplished the task by zigzagging. Once it was parked on the land, we spent some time trying to clean it out before we actually moved into it.

Unfortunately, it was not dry on the autumn day we moved onto the land. It was pouring rain. With extremely limited supplies and clothing, we crammed ourselves into the small trailer. There were two adults and seven children living in that small space, and I was pregnant with my eighth child.

The next morning, Jason slogged down the muddy hills to work; and during the day, it began to rain again. It was miserably cold and damp—there was no heat—and soon the rain began to drip on us inside the trailer. The children had nothing to keep busy with. The bathroom was not hooked up, so we put a bucket underneath the trailer where the toilet drained. It was some improvement over the ring of rocks on bare soil we had used when the well was being drilled. In the center part of the trailer, there was a small built-in dresser on one side and a compact set of bunks on the other; in the very back was a compartment with a small double bed that Jason and I used. The kitchen was tiny, and there was a diesel heater that didn't work. A mattress in the front living area served as a bed for the rest of the children who weren't sleeping in the bunks. We did our best to clean the trailer, but the ceiling tiles in the main part had mostly fallen off as a result of water damage. The whole space had a strong odor of mouse urine, especially in the dresser area, where we discovered mouse nests and drawers filled with feces and dead rodents. Sticky mouse droppings were all over the trailer.

Since there was no electricity, it was not only cold and dripping wet but dark, as well. I sat for several hours and tried to write. The minutes seemed endless. Dark, gloomy, wet. Time sputtered to a standstill. We tried to play games, but the mood was too bleak. The children huddled together under damp blankets as water dripped on them. Drops of rain mingled with tears. Hopelessness welled up in that small trailer. I decided that we were not going to do it; it was too hard. No one should be reduced to this state of misery. Imagine shivering with the cold, being wet without a place to get dry, having only peanut butter and jelly sandwiches to eat, and the acrid stench of mouse urine filling the air—then you will have an idea of what it was like.

Taking the oldest son, Ryan, with me, we tramped across the sodden hills toward the nearest neighbor to use their phone. I called Jason at work and asked him to come back; we were too cold and wet. While we were gone, Alex slammed his thumb in the trailer door, slicing it deeply. His fingers were numb with the cold. He wrapped his thumb with toilet paper and suffered while he waited for us to return. There was little I could do for Alex's thumb without a first aid kit. Jason finally arrived and brought with him a radio phone, a large, clunky thing that was fitted with a battery pack. It was one of the first mobile phones, cutting-edge technology at the time. At least I had something to call with, if we had another medical emergency, but poor Alex had no relief for his pain until it healed. Being cold and miserable didn't help matters. Soon after, we bought a first aid kit to have on hand.

Unless we moved all the way back to Aldridge, there was nowhere else for us to go. We had given up the rental and now had mortgage payments. Somehow, we made it through that day, and the next...

For quite some time, we ate peanut butter and jelly sandwiches, crackers, pretzels, and apples. I had no way of cooking anything—the kitchen stove didn't work, and there was no refrigeration or hot water. We couldn't start a fire in the trailer, and it was raining too much to start one outside. Besides, we had no wood. We were surrounded by forests in the distance, but they were all wet and uncut. Finally, Jason hauled in our old generator and hooked it up. He also bought some eggs, milk, and an ice chest. The ice didn't last long, but the eggs lasted pretty well, even without refrigeration.

The first hot meal was amazing. Jason cranked up the generator (it was an old military crank start) and plugged in a griddle. The jonny cakes browned on one side then I flipped them to crisp on the other side. Eggs sizzled in the butter, and then I served the jonny cakes with an egg perched on top and butter dripping down the sides. The over-easy eggs broke open as the children ate them, the yellow, eggy goodness covering everything like syrup on pancakes. The children formed a ring around me as I cooked and hungrily took their turns as the steaming feast came off the griddle. It was so wonderful to eat a hot meal that they couldn't get enough, especially after weeks of cold, starchy food.

Many years later, Aleena told me that, during those first weeks on the land, she ate so many peanut butter and jelly sandwiches that she dreamed one of the boys had turned into a peanut butter sandwich and gotten stuck under her bed.

To get in and out of the property, Jason basically slid down the hills with the Suburban, careening back and forth as he spun the wheel to correct it and keep it from overturning. It scared me to death, but the kids screamed with delight as if they were on a roller coaster. Jason made a deal with the neighbor, who worked with heavy equipment, to carve us out a road. Then he struck up another deal with a local rock-crushing company to haul in crushed rock. Within the first few months, we had a rough gravel road that snaked up across the hills from the county road to the highest point of the property.

* * *

One trailer was obviously not enough, so Jason asked around and found another abandoned trailer so far gone that no one wanted it. It was a fifty-by-ten-foot heap of scrap. The roof leaked in various places, including a large gaping hole over the kitchen, and mold covered everything. The oven and stove worked once we hooked up propane, but the rest of it needed a lot of work. Food had been left to rot in the refrigerator stunk, and the toilet had been used without benefit of water. There was dirt, mold, and filth caked everywhere;

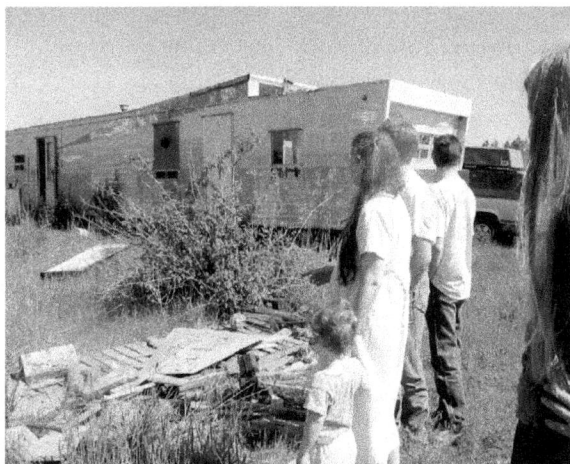

the smell was atrocious. Together, we cleaned out the trailer and hauled it onto the property. It was positioned near the back part of our land on the last hill before the property sloped steeply downward toward the forested section. We then moved the first trailer parallel to it with a walkway between the two trailers.

Next, we had to make the trailers livable. In the larger trailer, we ripped off the thin board walls down to the studs, and the bathroom was torn out completely. The children and I helped with the drywall, taping, mudding, painting, and all of the cleaning. Jason's boss, Darrel, also pitched in.

We bought an old used piece of carpet to cover the living room floor; it was more of a throw rug. The skinny hallway was bare plywood which was left uncarpeted. A set of bunk beds was forced into one of the tiny bedrooms, leaving barely enough room to turn around in. Somehow, we fit a king bed into the rear bedroom. A narrow path next to the bed gave access to an escape door on that same wall. Off the end of the bed were a shelf and a bar to hang clothes. Otherwise, the bed *was* the room, with just enough space on one side to stand and change clothes.

A full-sized couch fit in the living room but nothing else could be squeezed in except for a wood stove. There were two large windows over the back of the couch and a walking space between the couch and woodstove that led to the kitchen, with its stained rotted floor. A compact wooden table and two chairs fit in the kitchen under the

gaping hole. A piece of plastic sheeting was hung from the ceiling near the hole and slanted, so that the rain water was shunted into a bucket and then emptied. Although the propane oven and stove were only camping size, they were a great improvement over the generator-fueled griddle for making hot food. It was nice to be able to see out of the windows over the kitchen sink.

Going to the bathroom was a challenge. The bathroom was left unfinished and not hooked up to the septic or water; a bucket was available for emergencies, however. The boys decided to build an outhouse while their dad was at work. Even though I was proud of their efforts, their engineering needed a bit more guidance. When they were finished, you had to sit sideways with your feet almost out the door, because they did not leave enough room for knees.

Storage buckets were lined all around the drip line of the trailer to catch the rain, which was then used for bathing and washing dishes. Whenever it rained, we got a reprieve from lugging water up the hill from the well. That hike went straight up the steepest hill on the property and was often a slippery slope of mud.

The generator was set up so it could run lights or the griddle once in a while but had to be used sparingly, because we had to haul the diesel in, sometimes by foot. Propane tanks were procured to fuel the oven and burners. Once we got the propane in, I was finally able to fix hot meals on a regular basis. We retrieved some books from the stash pile in Darrel's garage and began homeschooling again. Kerosene lamps were used for lighting, but they cast poor light for reading and, even with the wicks trimmed, the lamp fumes were objectionable in such close quarters.

Before winter set in, we put in some landscaping trees, especially hybrid poplars and some maples. Flowers, rhubarb, and other vegetation were planted on the south-facing side of the trailers. On the high plateau, right next to the ravine that contained the pump, a grid was laid out for fifty fruit trees and fifty hazelnut bushes. They were fenced in to keep the deer out, but the hungry critters got in anyway. We also had the acreage seed drilled for hay, with timothy, clover and alfalfa. A deal had been struck with a local harvester, they seeded and would harvest, while we would get a percentage of the income.

Winter on the Mountain

Winter came on and the heavy rain turned to heavy snow. Soon, there were walls of snow along the trenches we had dug to the privy. We melted snow continuously to provide enough water for cooking, drinking, and bathing. It took all day long to melt and heat enough snow to fill the bathtub only partway; the whole family then shared the same bath water.

When Christmas drew near, the three oldest boys, Ryan, Alex, and Brent, trekked to the nine acres of trees on the far side of the property. There was a steep hill to navigate before reaching the trees. Then they spent a long time trying to find the perfect tree before digging it out from under the snow. The boys were giddy with the thought of bringing a tree home that mom and their younger siblings would like. They selected a tree that looked exceptional, even though one side was bare. They sawed it down and began the tedious process of dragging the reluctant tree up a hill, as it seemed to cling desperately to the snow with its branches.

The boys were exhausted by the time they reached the trailers but felt it had been worth their efforts, as everyone clapped and jumped up and down with excitement as soon they spied the tree being dragged up the hill. When Jason saw the tree, he grabbed a saw and cut off the bottom nine inches of trunk (which made up about one third of the weight of the tree, because it was so thick). The boys were a bit crestfallen when they saw that hauling up the whole weight of the tree had been unnecessary.

In no time, it was tucked into the corner by the couch; it was a good thing one side was bereft of branches because as it was—we had to smash it into the corner to fit. The children were soon filled with joyful anticipation and spent the day decorating the tree with homemade paper chains, cut snowflakes, ornaments made out of cardboard and little animals Aleena had sewn. Aleena was quite an expert at sewing up miniature dolls by hand. She spent many a long hour sewing, scrunched over on her bed or the couch. Monkeys, bears, pigs, rabbits, and all sorts of creatures were crafted by her clever fingers. Her stitches were fine, and the finished items were gifted to others. It was a fun way for her to occupy herself during the long winter days.

*   *   *

Sometimes, even with the woodstove going, the cold reached its greedy hands in through thin walls, doors, and windows. The glass would be covered with a beautiful glazing of crystalline patterns, as the moisture froze even on the inside. The water that had trickled down when it was a bit warmer, formed dams of mounded ice in the aluminum window tracks, much like stalagmites. Everyone huddled inside as the outside thermometer dipped below zero, and we blew dragon breath at each other.

After doing their schoolwork, the children sometimes played games, drew, or did some reading. Subtle shadows provoked dread in the late afternoon, as darkness descended early, and it became too dim to do fine work. No sewing or reading could be done; eyes would tire from the strain. There wasn't much to do after the sun had fled. We told stories, practiced Spanish, played word games, and fought boredom. Sometimes, we had petty fights and were irritable. Cabin fever was inevitable. During daylight, the older children would play outside and, when the snow was just right, the hills were amazing for sledding, although a bit steep. Other times, they made snow forts and piled up snowballs.

"Come and see my snowman, Mom!" yelled Joseph, with his flaming red cheeks and an excited smile. I pulled on my boots and jacket and made my way through the soft wet snow to see a fat misshapen blob with some rock eyes and a stick nose. My young son had removed his own scarf and wrapped it around the place most resembling a neck on the mound of snow. Benjamin, the youngest child, was still too small to play outside in the snow so I went back in, bundled him up, and brought him out to see his brother's snowman. He squealed with delight.

*　*　*

The older boys slept in the smaller trailer. Often, they woke to find snow piled on their blankets; it had sifted through the cracks in the rotten roof. Their diesel heater never did work, even though Jason took it apart and tried to fix it several times. So they huddled together with Rosie, a black shepherd dog, to keep them warm and wore their heavy winter clothes and jackets to bed, sometimes even their boots.

Rosie was Alex's first dog; she followed him everywhere and was his constant companion. We also had acquired a few chickens. They didn't have any place to stay out of the weather, except for under the trailers. Alex took care of the creatures; he made sure they got food scraps and scrounged under the muddy trailer to see if the hens had laid any eggs.

Although it snowed heavily through that first winter, unseasonable warmth came in late January, and the trees budded out way too early. The snow melted quickly, and then the rain came on. It rained steadily. It poured. We didn't know it then, but that winter turned out to be the year of the one-hundred-year flood. With the early snow melt off and torrential rains, the whole valley was drenched with so much water that farms and houses were inundated. There even came a day when Jason could not get out to go to work. We were up high and could see the devastation at the lower elevations. Fields were flooded, and farmhouses sat in the middle of newborn lakes.

DEAD BABY

His eyes were closed in his bluish face; his chest was still.
The whole top part of his head was missing.

I WOKE FROM A DREAM ABRUPTLY IN THE CHILLY DARKNESS. The fire in the stove had died down, and the temperature had plummeted. I lay quietly and stared into the darkness. In my dream, I had seen my unborn baby; the baby had no head. I shivered as I stroked my pregnant belly, which seemed small for the gestation date.

A few weeks later, on a cold January morning, everyone piled into the Suburban and went to town to do errands. We were used to spending long hours camped out in the car during doctor or dentist appointments or when other errands were necessary. Jason would have to take off work, so we would fit all appointments and errands we needed to do in the same day. So it was usually an all-day affair when we went to town. I made sure the kids had snuggle blankets, snacks, water, and something to read or schoolwork to do. That time, I had a prenatal visit with my doctor. The doctor was concerned about the small measurement of my fundus—something I had noticed, as well—so he made an appointment for an ultrasound at the hospital across the street for that same day.

I already knew what they would find.

The friendly, talkative ultrasound technician lubed up my belly and began the scan. As he ran the device over me, his voice trailed off and his face fell.

"I need to call in the radiologist," he said.

As he moved to leave the room, I murmured, "I already know what's wrong with my baby. There is no head."

The technician was visibly shocked. "How do you know that?" he asked. "There is no way you could know that." He left the room and brought back the radiologist.

The radiologist explained that the unborn child had anencephaly, and his entire skull and brain was missing; however, he had a brain stem, face, ears, and a neck. The radiologist wanted to know how I knew what was wrong with the baby.

"God showed me in a dream," I replied.

The radiologist stared at me.

Jason frowned. "She didn't tell me," he stated grimly, as he avoiding looking in my direction.

We returned to the car and silence, which was unusual for the children. They knew something was wrong. My eyes watered and heat shot up my back and neck as I explained to them that their new baby brother would not live long after he was born. While the other children peppered me with questions, my oldest son, Ryan, got very quiet and gazed out of the window into the gathering darkness.

When we were alone, Jason demanded to know what had happened, so I told him about God asking me for a child and my answer to Him. And how, just a few weeks earlier, I'd seen in a dream that the baby had no head. My dream was imperfect; he actually had no head from the brow upward. Jason had witnessed my weird dreams coming true before, so it wasn't new to him. I had dreamed of two unborn nephews dying a few years before, and that had come true, among other things.

Jason became enraged and yelled, "You had no right to say yes."

"If God asked me that question, I would have said no!"

He was very angry with me. He had a tender heart for babies... He raged and then cried bitterly.

I had never seen him cry.

He did not realize that the reason I said yes to God was the same reason I remained in a terrible marriage and endured his treatment. I tried to do what I thought was God's will and wanted to abide by my vows. "For better or for worse" meant that you stuck it out no matter how hard it got. I believed, strongly, that I had to accept my lot in life. Knowing that, Jason took advantage and played me like he played his banjo.

I closed off my emotions. On the one hand, I was stricken with grief. On the other, elation filled my heart at the thought that this one child would not have to suffer like the other children still *were* suffering. And then there was the guilt that I felt because I hadn't wanted to get pregnant again.

* * *

In spring, when my due date drew near, my parents made the very long trip from California to help out.

They were shocked by the primitive conditions we lived in.

My dad bought an Aladdin lamp with a mantle—what an amazing improvement! Instead of sitting in the dim trailer at night and making up word games or trying to keep occupied, we were able to read and draw. Dread of the long, dark evenings diminished somewhat. Grandma and Grandpa helped out, and their presence was a welcomed joy. Grandpa cut the boys' hair; grandma helped the girls learn to crochet and snuck the children candy. They took our family out for pizza! Going out to eat was a very rare treat. Together, we all waited for the dreaded day to arrive.

The baby moved and kicked vigorously. My belly was quite large by then. I rubbed his little body with my hands through my thinning abdominal wall. I hoped he could feel how much I loved him. I had been pressured by several people to have an abortion. There was no way I would ever consider killing my sweet baby. We were bonded. The warmth and love I gave him was the only thing he would ever know in his short existence, and I would not subject him to pain and horror for my own convenience. He was God's baby; God had asked for him.

The sad day arrived. I went into labor and made the trip to the hospital where the staff had been specially prepared for us. One of the nurses confided that she had hoped to be at the birth and had prayed for mother and child. My parents stayed with the other children, so I didn't have to worry about them. The labor was very difficult as there was no presenting part to open the birth passage. Finally, the doctor broke the membrane, and a torrent of amniotic fluid soaked the birth bed and splashed out onto the floor. It was as if a flood had burst forth; even the doctor was surprised. My stomach became quite small again. The baby had not been able to swallow and recycle the amniotic fluid while in the womb, so it had built up inside, making me look big. After many hours and much exertion, my baby boy was finally born. He was wiped clean and placed in my arms.

Jason baptized Nicholas Evan as he lay motionless in my lap, naked on a soft white towel. His eyes were closed in his bluish face; his chest was still. The whole top part of his head was missing. I stroked his little arms and legs while the doctor monitored his heartbeat.

After thirteen minutes, the doctor looked up at me and whispered softly, "He's gone."

It seemed to me that my little boy was still present; silently, I said goodbye to him. Then he was gone, terribly gone. He never moved — the birth had been too traumatic for him. His tiny face was purple and bruised from the force of passage. There was nothing above the brow except dark-red tissue. He had no brain. He was perfect in every other way, a beautiful baby. I was hollow inside and did not cry.

The nurses moved me into a new room to recuperate, if "recuperate" is even a word you can use after watching your baby die in your arms. As the door swung open, I saw that my baby had been placed in a hospital crib in my room. He was wrapped like a mummy in a blanket with his face showing. An attempt had been made to cover his terrible deformity with one of those soft little stretchy baby hats, but it had failed.

From my bed, I watched as some of the nurses and hospital personnel came in and asked if they could see him. One woman was visibly shocked. A terrible void kept me from crying along, as did the awful feeling of joy I experienced, knowing that this little one would never have to suffer like the others had. There is something terribly wrong when a mother has joy that her baby is dead. So terribly wrong. I was so far gone, though, that I couldn't even see it.

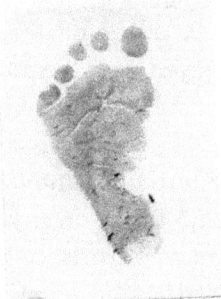

In the night, while going to the bathroom, I passed by his crib and glanced down at his lifeless body that still lay there in the crib. The dark face with jagged, blackened edges, where the skull should have been, sent a shock of horror through me. What was left of his face had bruised from his traumatic birth; it had turned purplish-black and looked withered in the darkness. Without a skull to protect it, the face had endured terrible force. It would have been nice if someone had thought to cover his face.

How much more will you ask of me God?

In the morning, a grief counselor came and tried to talk to me. She wanted me to cry. "Because it would help the process," she said.

A sense of unreality washed over me. She had no idea what I had been through, how deeply I had suffered, or even that I was happy Nicholas was with God. How do you tell someone you are happy that your baby is dead or that your grief is beyond tears? How could they understand from their safe, warm, comfortable world?

Later, two nurses came in and suggested I dress my baby for the trip home. The thought of holding his cold, stiff body and trying to force his little limbs into his baby clothes was something I couldn't do. So I asked them to do it for me. I watched as they dressed him and laid him in the bunting I had made for him. When they were done, they handed him to me. On the way home, as Jason drove, I sat in silence, holding my dead baby and wondering how many other women had driven back home holding a dead baby in their arms? Or maybe just as sad, how many had driven home with empty arms? I felt it was too much to ask any mother to endure.

To save money on a burial, Jason got permission to bring our baby's body home and bury him on the land. Then, with Ryan and Alex helping, he made a little coffin out of concrete and embedded a cross on the top of it.

Even before Nicholas' birth, the two eldest sons had been told, by Jason, to dig their baby brother's grave. Taking turns, they dug a dark muddy hole six feet down, way over their heads; it filled them with horror. They knew their very own baby brother would be buried in the hole they were digging. It was a terrible thing to ask boys to do. I felt that Jason should have dug the hole or hired someone else to do it.

When we arrived back, I laid Nicholas on my bed, and my mother came in to help me. I could not put the bonnet on him that I had knitted, because he had no head to put it on. Somehow, it had given me comfort to knit it anyway. I did not allow the children to see Nicholas, because he looked gruesome; they did not need the shock of seeing his shriveled, darkened face and missing skull as their only memory of him. I wrapped him in a blanket and laid him in his concrete casket. The children gave me little toys and things they had made for him, and I placed the items in the casket beside him. The concrete lid was placed on top, and he was sealed in.

Then, with our priest officiating and my parents and some friends attending, the small box was lowered into the deep hole on the seventy-six acres of sorrow. I still could not cry, but my heart broke.

Ryan and Alex had been forced to dig the terrible, deep wound in the earth, much to their horror. Yet I was blind to their suffering. I didn't notice Alex slink off as the priest began to bless the ground. I even asked Ryan to help my dad fill in the grave. He gave me a look of fear and backed away. If only time could be rewound, I would take him in my arms and comfort him. Then I would go find Alex, who ran off alone and cried bitterly.

But self-hatred will not repair that day.

My dad looked at me, the only one who seemed to be aware of what was transpiring. "I will do this," he said, as he continued to shovel the dark earth over my baby.

> *...smile. this one is for God. Yes, i know He loves me but*
> *He has so abandoned me. His eyes are closed, He must be*
> *on the cross still because I cannot reach him. my baby is*
> *with him. when I leaned my hand on the cross for support*
> *it came away covered in blood. Oh yes, blood. I know blood.*
> *Come after me.*
> *So i follow him, but I cry, i feel so abandoned, turn*
> *around and look at me, my god, love me and hug me in*

your big arms. I am with Him in the garden and god has
abandoned Him too. we hold hands and cry together. the
blood. the dead baby.
—*Excerpt from "Dead Baby," Tessy's writings, as written*

Grandpa carved a burial stone with the baby's name and the date of his birth and death. The stone was never used on the burial site. It now lies in California, in my family's outdoor shrine. The angel, called down by the priest to guard holy ground, still stands vigilant over an unmarked grave on the mountaintop where we all suffered so much. My mother and father returned to their home in California, and I was left to face Jason's grief and anger.

He took to drinking. When he drank too much whiskey, his emotions became exaggerated. He was morose and directed his rage at me. It was my fault the baby was dead. He accused me of not caring and not crying about the baby. I couldn't tell him how I really felt. He would never have understood.

His anger passed into denial. He asked everyone at work not to mention the baby's death. He did not want their sympathy. However, his company bought a tree, which we planted near the trailer, to honor Nicholas' death. It didn't help that the tree died the following winter.

Late Spring

Jason got up before dark, went to work early, and stayed late every day, often on Saturdays, as well. Yet he was salaried and didn't make more money by working overtime. I was left alone on the mountain with the children during the week, and we homeschooled. At sixteen, I had graduated with a GED (although I had attended a few art classes in college) and did not feel qualified to teach. Every year, before the school year started, I begged Jason to allow the kids to go to public school. I was stretched so thin and felt I could not go on.

I often wished the rest of us could go to work in a nice, warm, well-lit place with a real plumbed bathroom and a lunchroom handy. Occasionally, we did go with Jason and hung out in the break room at his place of employment. We would bring schoolwork and lunch and then spend most of the day there. Sometimes this happened when we had appointments in town; it would amaze me that his company was so generous by allowing it. For me and the children, the luxury of being in a comfortable place with a real toilet, running water, and lights was an incredible reprieve that we looked forward to.

When the rain finally stopped and the mud dried up, it was late spring. We had new chickens, and Rosie was intrigued. A great dog, she played with the children and tagged behind Alex as he romped around the property. Alex let her sleep in the bed he shared with his brother because she kept them warm. The dog and boy became inseparable.

The newly laid, rough gravel road that ran from the main county road to the highest place on the property ended far from where the trailers were. So we decided to move the trailers toward the road, not only for easier access, but so that we could see who was coming up our driveway and be closer to the well. We undertook the task of not only moving the two trailers but moving *everything*: plants, trees, privy, storage containers, etc. The privy had fallen down one night during some strong winds, and Uncle Bill had donated some lumber and plywood, so a new, larger privy had been built—with room for knees! It, too, would have to be moved.

The older boys and I uprooted and moved all of the landscaping trees and vegetation that had been planted around the trailers the prior fall. There were about twenty-five trees, several bushes, and other plants to move. It was a lot of work, but thankfully we did not have to move the orchard. The trailers were placed at a ninety-degree angle to each other so they had a "yard" between them.

Because there was nowhere else to put them, we lined the plastic food-storage buckets up against the back of the larger trailer. They sat exposed in the rain and the sun. As the sun warmed them, the dried beans and other grains—which had absorbed moisture—began to ferment, and sludge formed on the bottom of the bins. When there was deep snow outside, accessing the containers became very difficult. Not only did someone have to trudge through the snow, but crusted ice and mounded snow formed over the lids, so they had to be dug out to be accessed.

Therefore, the decision was made to build some sort of shelter for storage. With Ryan and Alex's help, Jason built a lean-to addition onto the large trailer. It helped keep the wind out and sheltered the front of the trailer, besides being a storage area. It was like an enclosed porch. I planted a climbing rose on the outside corner of the addition.

A new hole for the privy was dug out in the "yard." The old privy house was dragged from the former location and put over the hole.

Survivalists

As summer approached, we were still settling into the new location. Angela got her own kitty. It was black, and she named it Pepper. The two sisters played dress-up with the kitten, decking her out in doll clothes and having tea parties.

Jason decided he wanted to raise not only chickens but turkeys, too. There was no place to house them comfortably, so when the baby chicks and turkeys arrived, he put them in the trailer hallway. They were in their own box, but the noise and stench permeated our small living space. There wasn't enough room for the children, much less for loud chickens.

Once they were big enough, the fowl ran around outside and hid under the trailers. Aleena helped to take care of them and became attached to them, giving them names. The turkeys got too big to keep anywhere near the trailer, so they were moved to the fenced-in orchard, to give them some security. A tarp was wrapped around a fence corner to provide shelter, though it proved to be ridiculously inadequate. The poor things kept tightly bunched together for warmth and did not often leave their huddle.

When rain was scarce during warmer months, we hauled our drinking water by hand from the well far below, in the valley part of the hills. One day, Aleena was carrying up a gallon jug of water when her bare toes hit a dirt clod and peeled off the end layer of skin on her big toe. She screamed, and Ryan ran down the hill and piggy-backed her up the hill, her toe dripping with blood.

*   *   *

A child's plastic swimming pool was placed near the well pump, and sometimes, when it was hot, the children filled it with water and played in it or bathed in it, although it was very cold water.

During the warmer part of the year, we worked on fencing the property whenever we could. Our nearest neighbor was a drunkard and owned cows, but he had no land. Idaho has open-range laws that make it the home owner's duty to fence out the livestock, not the farmer's duty to fence them in. So our neighbor had been used to purchasing cattle and allowing his stock to roam on surrounding acreage that did not belong to him. We found our fence lines cut numerous times and the neighbor's cattle roaming on our property. Chasing the cows out and fixing the fence became a tedious, daily chore. The grasses that had been planted for hay flourished that year. As far as the eye could

see, the foothills were covered with timothy, clover, and alfalfa.

The children roamed the hills and played. They favored the small valleys where the hills plunged and a few trees had survived the clear-cutting at the bottom. One of the valleys had several mature trees and a grove of aspens. It was a perfect place to have fun, especially when a breeze set the aspen leaves to dancing. Then it became a magical place to lay out a small banquet on a picnic blanket and play pretend games. I liked walking down the drive and along the ridges; it was so beautiful in the summer.

Dirty laundry piled up in the bathtub until Friday, at which time Jason would take it to the laundromat in large, black garbage bags. By then, the clothes were usually moldy. Jason got tired of toting the stinky clothes, so he found an old wringer washer and brought it home for me to use. We needed to haul enough water to fill it, but it washed the clothes. Jason strung me some laundry lines, and I hung the wash out in the summer sun. I always enjoyed hanging the wash out. I loved being outdoors in the sun, smelling the fresh air and feeling the breeze. The oldest boys, then teens, took advantage of the harder-packed dirt, since it was no longer raining, and drove one of the smaller trucks around on the property. They had a few mishaps, which we didn't report to Jason, but when Ryan backed into a 2x4 and ran it through the rear cab window, Jason found out. He wasn't too upset about it, but he enrolled Ryan into a driver's training course in town. I wondered what his reaction would have been if it had been Aleena who had the mishap? ("See, I told you, women shouldn't drive.")

At the edge of the property was an old washed-out creek bed with a trickle of water left in it. So Jason took the three oldest boys there and tried to pan for gold, without success. Ryan and Alex often went poking around in the nearby forest; they usually didn't stray too far. There were neighbors dotted around the area, but since it was hilly and covered in forests, they were hard to find. One day, Ryan arrived home excited and out of breath. He described seeing a mother bear and two of her cubs in the forest. He had not stuck around, but instead had high-tailed it back home as fast as he could.

Yellow jackets seemed to be everywhere, and Joseph was allergic to them. Of course, he was the one they chased. Every sting he got seemed to have an incrementally worse reaction. Soon, the small stings resulted in swollen limbs and a huge red welt. I kept Benadryl on hand but worried about whether I could get him help in time, if he went into anaphylactic shock. Thankfully, that never happened.

Several of us dealt with different allergies. Ryan, Brent and

Benjamin were very allergic to cow's milk, and I had an allergy to mold. I had seizures in my younger years and had been diagnosed with borderline epilepsy. Certain medications or substances, like some grains, would make my brain swell. When that happened, the kids knew to watch out, because I would get very irritable and start screaming for no reason. I was not proud of myself when that happened.

The trailers were filled with mold, and I was often irritable, though probably not just from allergies. The last time I ever had a terrible fit like that was one morning when I was making breakfast, and Brent came in and accidentally dumped over a bowl filled with wet ingredients. I just snapped uncontrollably and began screaming at him. I finally stopped abruptly when I saw the look of fear and guilt in his eyes. I ran to my room and cried.

I would never, ever be a saint. It just wasn't going to happen.

Rosie the Shepherd Dog

The turkeys and chickens were getting bigger and running around the property. After one long day in a hot car doing errands, we arrived home to carnage. Rosie, the shepherd dog, apparently had killed several of the birds, including Aleena's favorite chicken. Perhaps the dog was thirsty or hungry; we weren't sure. Aleena held a funeral for her pets and buried them with many tears. A week later, a turkey was found dead, and then another, and another. The evidence pointed to Rosie, Alex's beloved dog. We were worried that the dog had gotten a taste for blood. Therefore, it was decided to put her down before she killed any other creatures.

Jason held Rosie by a leash, and he carried a gun.

"Come with me. It is time for you to learn to be a man," Jason called to Alex, who reluctantly followed his dad down a steep incline to the edge of the forest. There was a washed-out gully at the bottom of the hill filled with brush.

"You need to shoot your dog so she won't kill anymore chickens and turkeys or maybe even one of the children," Jason told him firmly.

Alex couldn't do it and refused.

A gunshot split the air and startled me. A few minutes later, Alex rushed in and stared at me with horror.

"Mom, Rosie's dead. Dad shot her."

That's when I found out that Jason had taken Alex to witness Rosie being shot. No, he actually *insisted* Alex shoot his own dog, so he could learn to "be a man." Alex had refused, so, right in front of Alex, who was just eleven, Jason blew her brains over the field brush with one shot.

If that's being a man, who would ever want to be a man?

How much horror can a boy take? I wondered. Most of his life had been spent suffering from terrible living conditions. He had been forced to dig his brother's grave, now he had to watch his beloved dog get her brains shot out? How bleak life must have seemed to Alex, especially at that moment, with his best friend's brains scattered amongst the weeds.

Improvements

The seasons rolled one into another; sometimes it seemed as if time stood still. We continued to make improvements to our living conditions. The neighbor who worked with heavy construction equipment dug us a cistern, which was a very large hole that would have held approximately ten thousand gallons of water. A trench was dug from the well at the bottom of the steep hill toward the cistern, at the top. Water lines were laid in the trench but did not yet connect the well to the cistern. A two-thousand-gallon septic system was also dug. As soon as we could, we planned to build forms and pour concrete.

Other improvements included installation of a new phone line and a gate at the bottom of the drive, by the road; work also continued on the fence.

It was very early on a Sunday spring morning, as we slowly drove down the steep, gravelly drive onto the county road, I gazed out the car window at the bleak hills, with their slushy ground cover. I felt sick to my stomach and reached for a slice of green apple from a sandwich bag in my lap. Sour green apples kept morning sickness at bay. The drive to town seemed to take forever, and the winding roads made me sick.

Our ninth child was due in January. It had been a year since Nicholas was born. Fleeting thoughts of my dead baby son, buried in the cold ground, flashed through my mind.

How much longer can I go on?

Grim determination kept me going, along with the hope that my children would finally have a nice warm, cozy home. Jason had promised. It was the dream he had held out to me over and over, like a prize that kept being snatched away as soon as I got close enough. It was like an object in my peripheral vision that disappeared once I turned to look right at it. I really did believe he would build us a nice home—he had the skills, I knew he *could* do it. Although, in retrospect, I should have known better. In our other homes, he had never fixed them or made them more comfortable for us, but had played his banjo in his spare time, instead.

Jason had promised us that, if we stuck it out for three years, we would have a beautiful house built by all of us working together. He had mulled over how to make the structure using a handmade "Lego"-type of concrete brick. It could not be a standard house; it had to be unusual. He wanted to build molds to make the fitted bricks. He also looked into rammed-earth or hay-bale construction. The cistern and septic holes, which the earth-movers had dug out the previous fall, had fallen in with heavy mud during the rains. We could not ask our neighbor to dig them out again—it had been a big enough favor the first time. So, while Jason went to work each day, Ryan, Alex, and I jerry-rigged a setup with a wagon and inclined rails to haul the dirt back out of the deep holes. The work was hard, and it took us months to accomplish. After the cistern, we worked on the septic system with its enormous drain field.

As the work on the holes progressed, Jason showed the boys how to build the forms, which would hold the concrete when the sides were poured. This work took all spring and summer. Finally, we were ready for the concrete to be poured. A massive concrete truck showed up early one morning. It was fascinating to see the finished wall of concrete, once the forms were removed. Although it now had sides, the cistern did not yet have a lid, so the boys laid boards across the deep hole to keep the little ones from falling in.

After the concrete was poured, the next project was building a coop to keep the chickens from cannibalizing each other. Such behavior was caused by poor health due to their constantly being wet and cold. The turkeys were gone, all killed or dead from exposure. The orchard trees had been vandalized by the deer — the young trees were like candy to them.

The really difficult work during the summer months was to haul enough water up the steep hill to the orchard to water the fifty trees and hazelnut bushes. Being pregnant, I tired easily, but I didn't feel right to me, having the children do all of the hard work. My sons tried to dissuade me, but I helped them anyway. I always figured it was better to work alongside them rather than their working alone and losing heart. It was a never-ending chore, and a rare summer rain was very welcomed. The amount of water the small trees received was not enough to help them thrive. It was just enough to keep them alive. It was kind of like love: when you only get enough to survive but not thrive, you can become stunted.

As my pregnancy progressed, I felt sad for this new child in my womb. Life would be hard for him or her. I didn't understand how a baby would do well in a trailer where I couldn't put him down on the floor to learn to crawl. Jason bought some tile and tiled the kitchen and bathroom, but the hallway was still bare splintered ply board, and the rug we put in the living room had become caked in dried mud.

Bringing in Supplies

We were housebound by heavy snowfall the following winter. To get to work each morning, Jason strapped on snowshoes and trudged down the mountain to his car, which he parked on the county road about a mile from the trailers. Lucky for us, the road was kept ploughed to accommodate the school bus. Bringing back supplies was a daunting task until Jason came up with the dog sled idea. His boss had a kennel and raced huskies for sport. However, it wasn't dogs Jason used to pull the sledge; he strapped in our children. Loaded with groceries and fuel, they dragged their heavy burden up the first hill. Heavy snow made the going rough. Once they crested the hill and began the descent on the north-facing side, the weighted sled gained momentum. The older children were able to outrun it, but Alex tripped and was plowed under. He was cold and shaken, but the depth of the snow and the length of the sledge runners allowed it to pass safely above him. It's not every day you can plant your face in the snow and get run over by the supplies. Poor Alex, he had more than his fair share of mishaps. I hugged him and helped him off with his snow-coated jacket and scarf.

It was torture to use the privy, especially at night when it was fourteen degrees outside. I would leave my warmish bed, stumble down the crooked stack of bricks, and putter across the hard snow. Shivering, I crossed my arms around myself tightly. Since nothing was done to moderate the odor, the smell was offensive and overpowering. After sitting down on the cold seat, I heard it: the crackling, sucking sounds. I jumped up scared, with the feeling that a clammy hand was going to reach up through the endless pit underneath my butt and touch my exposed bottom. My flashlight was handy, so I could see in the dark. Peering down into the dark hole, I saw them. *Maggots*. Large, brown-headed maggots roiling in the human waste; horrifyingly, they also crawled up the sides of the excrement-lined hole. My stomach twisted as I shuddered with revulsion. If I had been a kid, I might have preferred peeing the bed rather than return to the maggoty privy. Maybe I would have gotten punished, but I would have been safe and warm, at least until I moved and felt the icy wetness against my skin. We all looked forward to the day when the septic was hooked up to the bathroom and we could use a normal toilet again.

*   *   *

Jason brought home a new dog for Alex, an Australian shepherd named Misty. She was pregnant and had a litter of puppies during the winter. She didn't like being a mother or nursing her babies. I found out she was birthing her litter when I heard a high-pitched wailing from outside and went to investigate. I found a newborn pup lying outside on the frozen snow, shivering and crying piteously. I called Alex, who promptly made Misty a warm spot to finish having her brood. She had three pups and nursed them reluctantly, often leaving them hungry. Alex took over feeding them and found them homes. But he kept one puppy that he named Max. So then we had two dogs plus a black cat named Pepper and some chickens.

* * *

By Christmas, the snow had melted enough for us to get out again, which was a good thing because, on January 1st, I bore my ninth child. He had a huge head covered with the most beautiful copper-penny colored hair. His large skull diameter, listlessness, and lack of muscle tone were noted by the doctor. Although he was the first baby born in the county that year, there was no newspaper fanfare or merchant baby gifts for him, as that tradition had been discontinued the year before.

When we brought our new son, Jon, home from the hospital, I laid him in a plastic rectangular storage bucket that served as a baby bed. I was able to squeeze it into the space between my bed and the wall near the tiny back door. Jon was a winter baby, and, with the crowded conditions in the trailer, he spent most of his time in the back room. Life continued with homeschooling, playing outside in the snow, chores, reading, or sewing until around three in the afternoon and then stories, jokes, or word games in the evenings. The children didn't get to see Jason often because he arrived long after their bed time and left very early in the mornings.

* * *

As spring inched forward and the rainy season commenced, we were mostly confined indoors again. The rainwater poured in over the kitchen table and was shunted down into the bucket reserved for it. I taught my kindergarten-aged son, Joseph, how to read at that same table to the sound of cascading water. Joseph was always trying to do things for his mamma. I fondly remember a bright spring day, the ground still covered by snow, when he called for me to come out to see a surprise he was working on. I dressed in warm clothes and boots and went outside. He was bundled up, his flaming red cheeks peeking above his scarf, busily working with a snow shovel. He was moving all of the snow from the large area behind the trailer, an area that sloped uphill and was heavily laden with snow.

"Look, Mom," he said with shiny eyes and a big grin. "I am moving all of the snow for you so it won't melt and get the yard all muddy."

I smiled and hugged him. I didn't have the heart to tell him that, once it melted on the slope and property above, no amount of removal would keep the ground from getting muddy. Imagine the floor near the front door with nine pairs of muddy boots, and you will understand why the mud could be a problem.

The larger trailer was the only living space that was warm, so the children crammed onto the couch, which was directly in front of the fire stove, and did their schoolwork. The girls often sat on their bed to read, sew, or work on their school papers. A single couch fit into the confined space in the living room, so we also used the two chairs at the small kitchen table. I usually sat or lay on the bed in the back room with the baby after breakfast was done. It was very hard to pass the long days with so little to do. I would hold the baby and read or help the kids with their schooling. It wasn't always that way—sometimes there was a project that would break up the monotony. Once, it was hooking up the septic system.

During the day, after the school work was finished, Alex and I would put on our rain jackets and work on digging the final trench which would hook the toilet in the trailer to the septic system. Aleena watched the baby for me, and the other children perched on the couch and watched us from the window. Our team effort was rewarded by our being able to use a real toilet! Containers of cistern water were then stored near the toilet, to wash it down after use. For us, it was a major step forward.

Early on Saturday mornings, we would prepare for baths because it took most of the day to accomplish the task. There was a tub in the tiny cramped bathroom, but no running water. The cistern was filled partway with runoff from the rains, so the boys would slide over the makeshift lid of the cistern and haul up water. These were carried to the living room woodstove and poured into large metal pots that were crowded on top to heat. After four to six hours, the water would be warm enough to fill the bath about six inches deep. I bathed first, Jason got in after me, and then the girls and younger children got into an ever-dirtier bath. Last, the older boys would bathe. By the time the unfortunate final child got in, the water was chilled and dirty with scum, with hair mazes floating on the surface. It was tough being a boy in our family.

One day, I was outside near the cistern and decided to look inside to see how much water was left. I lifted the lid and shuddered in disgust to see leaves, debris, bugs, and bloated rat corpses floating in the water. After that, we still used the water for bathing and watering plants, but I had Ryan and Alex scoop out the dead rodents. We didn't have much choice: it was just too much work to haul enough fresh water up the hill from the pump to bathe with.

Resolution

Summer showed up with determination. By then, Ryan was commuting with his dad to work, after being offered a job at the same company. He had finished his schooling by passing the GED and was employed by Aquatronics as a programmer.

The boys set up a large tent as a shelter and playhouse for the younger children to use during the day when it was hot. They ended up virtually living in it, since it was cooler to sleep in than the hot trailers at night. It was also fun to throw sleeping bags out on the ground and watch the stars after a marshmallow roast around a crackling fire built within a circle of rocks. The rare summer storms were also entertaining to view as they rolled in. There was a good vantage point from the front yard, using some makeshift chairs and a hammock strung between posts on the addition.

It was nice to be outdoors in the early morning and evening, but in the heat of the day, I stayed in trailer with the baby. There was nowhere a baby could go when it was hot outside, with the sun directly overhead. He fussed and cried, and I tried to keep him cool with wet cloths and a paper fan. Even with the windows and doors open, it was terribly hot, plus, the open doors allowed the yellow jackets to get inside. There were times I felt sorry for the both of us, as I sat hour after hour on the bed with my fussy baby, sweat rolling down my sticky skin. I cried out to God, but he didn't seem to care. I hated to see my kids suffer. Jason didn't really notice—he was at work ten to twelve or more hours a day in an air-conditioned building. And I was jealous of that.

*　　*　　*

We continued to repair the fence that ran between us and our drunk-ard neighbor to the south, who still cut the wires daily to allow his cattle access to our acres of hay grasses. Sometimes we drove behind him on the county road and would see him toss beer cans out of his window, littering the sides of the road.

The harvestable amount of hay that year was less than the year before, so we allowed it to grow without harvesting it. We did not want to have a repeat of the year before, when our fence-cutting neighbor drove in and loaded his truck with several tons of baled hay without permission, and the harvester lied to us about the harvest amount then cut us out of the proceeds. The harvester came and asked to bale again, but we turned him away. Better to let it go than let thieves have their way.

I scanned the property from the vantage point of the highest ridge. It was so beautiful. I could spy sparkling fool's gold embedded on the sides of the hills where the topsoil had worn away and could see the pump, down in the crack between the ridge and the next hill. *So* many gallons of water had been hauled from that pump, up the steep incline. We worked hard for *so* long in anticipation of our own home. It started back in that small trailer in my parent's orchard (where I first realized what a terrible mistake I had made), then in the mouse house, the old Aldridge house, the rentals, and finally in the mountain place. Even though it was beautiful, I couldn't bring myself to call it home even after all those years. There was still no house on it; not yet, anyway.

*   *   *

As summer faded, we closed in on the three-year mark. And I finally came to the realization that there would be no house. Jason still talked vaguely about making his own cement blocks to build a fitted-block-type house or maybe a hay-bale house, but it was just talk to put me off. I had been so damn gullible. He'd put no real effort into starting the actual house, and I realized he was dragging his feet. At that point, it occurred to me that there was even a lack of progress on the other projects, as well, including finishing the fencing and getting the cistern hooked up with a proper lid. I confided in some friends of ours from church, Marlene and her husband, who invited us over once in a while for home-cooked meals and hot showers when we were in town for church. They knew of our situation.

Marlene's husband said something that shocked me. "You are to blame if this situation continues," he stated firmly and with conviction. I was confused, not understanding what he meant by that statement. He continued, "You alone can end the suffering you and your children are enduring. You have to put your foot down and tell him to take you back to Aldridge. Tell him that you will not put up with the situation any longer."

Usually, the group of Catholics we were around would have encouraged me to do whatever my husband wanted. I felt numb. The man was right. I just never had it pointed out to me so clearly and bluntly. Someone else's objectivity shattered the illusion that I had been doing the right thing by going along with this terrible situation.

The children had suffered enough. Burying their baby brother, digging wells and cisterns, bathing in dirty water, carrying our drinking water up steep hills, being isolated without friends, having no electricity or refrigeration, suffering bitter cold without a heater, having snow fall on their beds, hauling in groceries by sled like dogs, watching their beloved pet get her brains blown out... It was too much. Why had I allowed this situation to continue for so long? What kind of horror story were we stuck in?

I kept everyone going with the repeated encouragement, "If we work hard, we will have a nice home within three years." I flushed with shame and berated myself bitterly.

Jason had no intention of ever building a house. He never had and was probably content with living the way we were.

Hearing the truth from someone else gave me courage I didn't know I had. I confronted Jason and told him I saw no end in sight, no house in the works, and I wanted to take the children back to the house in Aldridge. Surprisingly, he gave me no resistance—he almost seemed relieved. It had been his dream, but he wasn't really the one living it, since he spent most of his waking hours at work.

So we packed up our stuff and headed back to Aldridge.

Upon that cold mountain, we left behind not only three years of suffering and useless toil, but our infant son, forever guarded by the angel standing vigil over that holy piece of ground. As we made our way down the winding beer-can-littered county road, we bade our grim and silent goodbyes. The drunkard neighbor was happy, as he cut the fences once again. With our family gone, his cows had free range.

CHAPTER 5:
DECADE 3—YEAR 2000

ALDRIDGE AGAIN

*I realized with a wild tearing of my heart that if I had not
checked on him one more time before leaving, he would have
been dead when I returned.*

AS WE MADE OUR WAY BACK TO OUR ALDRIDGE HOME, we had become a
family of ten (not counting Nicholas). The ancient clapboard house
looked neglected. We discovered that drug squatters had used the
empty house in ourh
ABSENCE. IT was a complete mess, and everything of any value had
been stolen.

Baby Jon was almost accidentally suffocated to death right after
we arrived back. It was such a close call that my heart catches whenever I think about it.

We had arrived in Aldridge after the long trip home and immediately began unloading. There was a mattress lying on the floor in the
front room, so I laid the baby on the mattress because he had fallen
asleep on the long drive. I thought that a walk to stretch my legs

would feel good after sitting in the car all day. The small local store was only a few blocks away, and I needed to pick up a few things. The boys were unloading the Suburban and throwing things down in piles. I asked the children to watch the baby while I was gone, and then I made a restroom visit. I decided to check on the baby one more time before we left. Jason was going to accompany me.

When I returned to the living room, I stopped and stared at the mattress. It was piled high with blankets, pillows, and sleeping bags. I stood frozen for a moment and could not figure out where the baby was.

Then frantically I began screaming as I tore off layers of bedding, "Where is the baby? Where did you put him? *Where is he?*"

The boys stopped in their tracks, stunned. They had piled the bedding on top of the baby without seeing him lying there, wrapped in his own blanket. *What was going on? What was wrong? Why was mom screaming?*

I got to the bottom of the pile and there was my sweet little red-headed baby. He was barely breathing and covered in large drops of sweat. I caught him up, hugged him tightly, and loosened his clothes as he began to breathe easier and cry. I realized with a wild tearing of my heart that if I had not checked on him one more time before leaving, he would have been dead when I returned. *How do children survive childhood? How?*

* * *

Jason began commuting back to his job in Fuller, and this time, he took not only Ryan with him, but Alex, our second-oldest son, as well. Both of them now had jobs at Aquatronics, Inc. Two of my best helpers would now be gone. My oldest sons and I had borne the brunt of the hard outside work at each of the houses as well as on the seventy-six acres. Together we'd painted, mowed, taken out garbage, dug out a cistern and septic field, raked leaves, planted an orchard, taken care of chickens and turkeys, landscaped, dry-walled, mudded, textured, hauled water and firewood, cleared snow, and whatever else needed to be done during the workweek, while Jason was gone (and while he was at home). Aleena helped make that possible by caring for the younger children so I could get out and do the work.

Once we returned to Aldridge, my two older sons would be gone.

> *A couple years later, as a teen, I ended up getting a job at the place where my dad and older brother worked. My dad was borrowing a small trailer from a co-worker that he slept in out in the parking lot. We commuted to work very early Monday morning, and returned home on Thursday evening. We had to commute about four and a half hours. Well, there wasn't enough room in this small trailer, and my dad wasn't about to get me some place to sleep. I remember that it was almost winter and pouring down ice cold rain. I had no place to sleep, so I would go through the cardboard dumpster at work and build a small tent out of cardboard every night. I would hardly sleep through being wet and cold. Very early every morning I would have to get up and break down my cardboard shelter and put it back in the cardboard dumpster before anybody showed up to work...*
> —*Excerpt from* My Life *by Alex Gannon*

Facing Death – My Last Baby

> *As he examined me, he got serious and said quietly, "There is a whole unit of blood here." Emerging from me was a clot the size of a unit of blood. He looked at me and said, "This baby needs to be born now..."*

The seasons had rolled one into another. My old companions, depression and despair clung tenaciously. Life seemed so bleak at times, especially when winter came on. I could see no end to the childbearing and subpar living conditions. I struggled emotionally to hang on while trying to make life happy for my children. Jason was emotionally detached and had no empathy for me—or anyone, for that matter.

I once confessed to him that I sometimes felt I could not go on and had suicidal thoughts.

He looked at me coldly and, with a cruel voice, replied, "We all feel that way at times. Get over it." Somehow, I still hoped that he would care. (My imagination: "Honey, let's see what we can do to make things easier for you, you shouldn't be feeling so low.")Feeling unloved and unappreciated was the hardest thing to bear. If I had felt loved, I could have endured anything (and was doing a pretty damn good job of enduring even being unloved). But suffering endlessly for no purpose was dehumanizing and brought on despair. There seemed no hope left.

In the summer of 2000, I found out I was pregnant with my tenth child (Nicholas had been the eighth, Jon, the ninth). The baby was due at the end of March of the following year. The pregnancy tried my soul to the breaking point.

The words Jason had spat at me earlier in our marriage echoed in my heart. *You can have baby after baby until you almost die, and then the doctors will take care of it.*

He also told me once that I was *never* to get "sliced."

"If anything ever goes wrong, the baby will have to die," he had instructed me in a conversation long ago. Then he'd added adamantly, "I do not want a sliced wife. We can always have more babies."

Funny how life makes you eat your words.

I cried out to God. Since using birth control was against Catholic beliefs, and Jason would not cooperate with Natural Family Planning, I felt as if I had only three choices: kill myself, kill him, or run away. I could never have abandoned my sweet babies. They were the reason I had held on for so many years. I also realized I would never, could never, kill anyone.

So once again, with a terrible rending of my soul, I surrendered to God and said, "Your will be done." Once I surrendered, I felt some peace and went about trying to make a home for the children. I did have another talk with God, though. I let him know that nine months was too long to be pregnant, and that since I didn't have a husband who loved or cared about me, God would have to take care of me. I expected Him to put an end to my childbearing one way or another, and I let Him know it.

Winter reared its ugly head once again. We laid in firewood and caulked windows. I knitted more mittens. I also sewed up some soft polar fleece mittens covered with a waterproof fabric, which was much better at keeping little hands warm than the knitted mittens.

I hid my pregnancy from the neighbors, because I didn't want to hear their remarks about having too many children or the "hasn't she learned how that happens yet?" comments. Most people were nice to me, but I just didn't want to deal with nasty people at that time. I got bigger as winter came on, but it wasn't too hard to wear a jacket to hide my growing body. I didn't get out much, anyway. I sewed Barbie clothes for the girls so they could have fun playing with their dolls.

"Play with us, Mom!" they would beg, but for some reason, I just couldn't play. Instead, I sat near them and made clothes for their dolls. The smaller boys made forts inside and played hide 'n go seek in the dark when evening fell or were happy to get out in the snow, slide on their saucer sleds, make snow igloos, and lick icicles, which broke off from the eaves.

As my pregnancy progressed, we made a few trips up north with Jason, so I could get some prenatal care. Often we would make the long trip, stay camped out in the car or hang around the break room at work, and then, after my appointment, we would drive back home, since we had nowhere to stay and hotel rooms were not even a consideration. Jason would then take work home so he didn't fall behind. His company was amazingly flexible with his schedule and allowed us to hang out in the breakroom at work.

One such time, it was late fall around Thanksgiving. We had spent the day in the car, my belly was getting big enough to be in the way, I was exhausted, and my feet hurt. The company VP invited us to dinner with him and his family. After my appointment, Jason took us to their house early, because there was nowhere else for us to go. We showed up with all of the children who were disheveled and hungry.

Then, an act of extreme kindness was shown to me that I will never forget.

The VP's wife took one look at me, carrying my two-year-old developmentally delayed son and my pregnant stomach and observed, "I bet you're tired."

I nodded and smiled back. "Yes, I haven't been able to lie down all day." Then she took my arm with a sweet smile and, without another word, guided me into her own bedroom and put me and my toddler into her own bed!

"Don't worry about the kids, we have games they can play," she whispered as she closed the door.

Grateful, I took a nap with Jon curled up beside me. Later, we had a lovely dinner, and my children had a wonderful time playing with her children. I had never met this gentle kind woman before, but she treated me like a family member.

Her act of kindness changed something in me. There was a shift, a realization that people could be and should be kind to others. The hardened shell I had built up over the years for deflecting emotional pain softened somewhat, and I tried from that from that time forward, to be more charitable to others.

*   *   *

Christmas was over. There was a jumble of wrappings and abandoned Christmas stockings strewn randomly around the house. We had a nice family buffet on Christmas Eve. I baked a ham and made Boston Baked beans; we had a spread of nuts, cheeses, home-baked cookies, and fudge, plus the family favorite, Kirschkuchen, a Christmas cake made with raisins, walnuts, and maraschino cherries. Since Jason's parents now lived close by, having moved from California several years earlier, they came over to share the buffet with us. The children were happy with their small gifts, lovingly handmade or bought and hidden during the months preceding the holiday.

I went to bed that Christmas night not realizing my life would change in a few hours.

In the wee hours of the morning, around 2 a.m., I woke up to a gush of hot blood between my legs, and then contractions started. I was six months pregnant. Our insurance only covered us in the Canton-Fuller area—where Jason still worked. It was a four-hour drive north on frozen roads. How lucky for me that Jason was home for Christmas and that his parents lived right down the street. The long drive to my doctor's seemed to last forever. I felt weird, got flushed, continued to hemorrhage, and had light contractions.

Once we arrived, my doctor had me check into the hospital right away, and I was given medication to stop the contractions and shots to mature the baby's lungs. An ultrasound was performed, and it was discovered that I had a complete placenta previa. The placenta was trying to pull away from the uterine wall, as my uterus began the last trimester stretching. I spent the next two weeks in the hospital, bedridden; I was not allowed to move. I could not get out of bed, even to go to the bathroom or shower. I had a copy of *War and Peace*, and my son Ryan had given me the *Mutiny on the Bounty* trilogy for Christmas. I never had so much rest in my life. I got to spend my time reading, working puzzles, and watching TV—we didn't *have* television at home. The medical shows were my favorite. I visited with the nurses, who all became my friends. Each one of them, one by one, came in and told me her life story. I loved spending time around other women and having the chance to talk and share with them.

After two weeks, the doctor allowed me to move into a hotel within five minutes' drive of the hospital. Jason brought a few of the children up to live with us in the hotel. I sure had missed them. Some of the children had to stay with Jason's parents, because there wasn't enough space in the hotel room. My baby son Jon had just turned three years old and had his own baby doll in tow. He was a smart little boy, but he lagged behind in normal development. He had not spoken even one word yet. We later found out he had autism. (Both of my children, born with neurological problems, had been conceived in the chemical-drenched western Washington wheat-growing area.)

I spent most of my time lying around and seemed to be recovering.

One evening, Jason took me to a company dinner (close to the hospital); we left the big kids in charge of the little ones. During dinner, we got a call that the emergency vehicles were at the hotel, and we needed to come right away. I can't describe the extreme emotions a parent experiences when they hear those awful words without knowing what has happened…

In terrible dread, my heart racing and my body flushing, we arrived back to find that Benjamin had been chasing Jon around the room, and Jon had fallen and hit his mouth on the corner of the lampstand. There were tooth marks in the wood. Two of his teeth had been driven back into the gums: one was torn out completely, and the other one was knocked sideways. When I saw him, he looked at me with a bleeding mouth and giggled hysterically as I folded him in my arms. The emergency crew was worried that he had hit his face so hard there might be more damage than was showing, so they wanted us to watch him. We took him and his torn-out tooth (in a cup of milk) to get checked by the dentist. The dentist replaced his tooth and felt he was okay.

Later the next day, I began to hemorrhage again. I went to the hospital, and they stabilized me as we waited for the doctor to come in and check me. He was in another emergency surgery, and it was also his birthday. His birthday had been filled with emergencies, and he was missing out on his own celebration. It was late when he came in; he looked exhausted. We joked about me having this baby on his birthday.

As he examined me, he got serious and said quietly, "There is a whole unit of blood here." Emerging from me was a clot the size of a unit of blood. He looked at me and said, "This baby needs to be born *now*." He reassured us and then left the room. Seconds later, a crew of nurses and attendants swarmed in, and the room was charged with urgency. They quickly prepped me for emergency surgery and wheeled me into the operating room.

*   *   *

Jason shook my shoulder and pestered me to wake up. I didn't want to wake up; I wanted him to leave me alone. We had agreed he would try to wake me up after surgery, since I didn't handle medications well and wasn't sure how I would handle general anesthesia.

After what seemed like hours, I finally got into a wheelchair and was wheeled into the nursery. My baby looked tiny in her incubator. She weighed about five pounds, a good size for a baby born at seven months gestation. She was skinny and looked like a little old lady; she had deeply yellowed skin. It wasn't too long until I could hold her, but I was too weak to hold her for long. This little one in my arms was to be my last baby, and we named her Misha. I teased her as she got older that she was the last one to slip through the gate; it was locked after she made it through. She is such a treasure. I then had seven sons and three daughters. Only Brent guessed that she would be a girl; the rest of us were sure that there would be another boy added to the family.

When we were finally able to take her to the hotel with us, we had to take an "outer space" light bed for her. She needed to sleep in it every day for hours, to help clear out the bilirubin that her liver couldn't get rid of.

Jon was ecstatic about his new baby sister. He assumed that she belonged to him, and he didn't like the other children getting near her or kissing her. We were still staying in the hotel room at that point. Each day, when the older boys got off of work, they tried to come in to see her and give her a kiss. Jon would stand guard and not let them by. Everyone thought it was kind of cute.

The doctor said I had lost at least four units of blood total over the weeks I had hemorrhaged. I not only had a wound across my lower abdomen, I also had a tubal ligation. While in surgery, my doctor discovered that even though the placenta obstructed the cervix, it also was so high on the uterus that he had to make an incision at the top of the uterus. He felt, after ten pregnancies and the high cut, my chance of having a ruptured uterus from any subsequent pregnancies was very likely, so—with our consent—he sterilized me. Not only was my fertility problem taken care of, but I also had my baby at seven months.

As you might remember, I let God know that I felt nine months was too long to be pregnant. I think He was having a gentle laugh.

Fired

> *"Jason wanted to be the star player at work and expected special treatment. He didn't want to follow the rules everyone else had to follow, and he wanted his children exempted, as well."*
>
> —*CEO of Aquatronics*

When we returned to Aldridge with our new baby, the townsfolk were astonished. We had left suddenly a month before, and when we returned, I had a new baby in my arms. As far as they knew, I wasn't even pregnant. Gossip flew.

Within six months, we packed up and moved to Fuller, Washington. Jason had found a house for us to purchase within three minutes' drive of where he worked. It was a nice, modest house of two thousand square feet with plenty of room for us. It had been a duplex, but we turned it back into a single-family home. I was very happy to move into a real house. Pergo floors covered the upstairs, the walls were painted and smooth, there was a real kitchen and plenty of room for the children. It was about a mile walk to town and a fifteen minute walk to where Jason and the older children worked—both Aleena and Brent also worked at Aquatronics by that time.

We lived in Fuller for two years, with mounting tension at Jason's workplace. According to the president of the company, Jason wanted to be the star player at work and expected special treatment. He didn't want to follow the rules everyone else had to follow, and he wanted his four children exempted, as well. Jason felt that our children should be exempt because they had been homeschooled and were smarter than the other employees; he also thought they should be compensated accordingly.

The business had been a family startup and became very

successful. They not only funded their own children's college edu-
cations, but they also encouraged and helped all of the young adults
who worked for them, so they could attend college. They offered
monetary help and work scheduling around classes. My children
finally had the hope of a college education. But Jason did not want
his children to attend college. He believed it was an unnecessary
waste of time and would ruin them. (He had been a ninth-grade
dropout.) I encouraged the children to attend college anyway, but
Jason's personality was too strong for the children to go against. So
that opportunity slipped away. Later, some of them would bitterly
regret the lost opportunity, when they discovered how hard it could
be to get decent jobs without an education.

About this time, Aleena decided, with grim determination, that
she wanted to drive and not turn out like me, a woman stuck at
home. She asked for help from her father and a few of the guys from
work. They went along with the teaching but then ridiculed and
made fun of her. Even though I was encouraging, her self-esteem
took a hit, and she decided she didn't have enough courage to follow
through. She had heard her whole life how women were bad drivers
and should not be on the road; I was not a good role model.

Then, one day, a female co-worker about Aleena's age took her
under wing and not only showed her how to drive safely; she went
driving with her until Aleena was able to get her license! Aleena's
face beamed with pride when she walked through the door with
her license in her hand. I was so proud of her that day, not only for
getting her license but for not giving into the sexist pressure around
her that said a woman shouldn't drive.

The middle children continued to homeschool, while Jon and
Misha played outdoors when the weather permitted. Jon still
behaved in an unusual manner, but we didn't yet know why.
Whenever he got hurt in a bad way, he didn't seem to notice, or he
laughed it off. Once, he hit his head on the concrete walk so hard
that he had a lump the size of a tootsie pop, but he didn't seem
concerned. A few months after we moved, he was playing in the
backyard, and Benjamin ran in to relay that Jon had pulled a tooth

out of his mouth, flung it away, and had run away laughing. It was the tooth he had damaged in the hotel incident. However, a very small, insignificant hurt would obsess and upset him quite a bit.

He was very young but easily memorized passwords if he saw them typed in; he loved computers or any electronic device. He was around three when, after not speaking a single word up to that point, he began to talk in sentences. But he was still very taciturn. He taught himself to read, but I didn't realize it until he read out loud the words from a poster hanging on a friend's wall. He was picky about his food and would only wear soft clothes. Loud sounds and frantic activity bothered him, so we couldn't take him into crowded or noisy places.

Misha and Jon were inseparable; they spent all of their time together. Misha was an angel with huge blue eyes and tightly wound natural curls. With her sweet gentle nature, she was every-one's favorite and quite the momma's girl. How sad we all were the day she pranced into the living room, shorn of her beautiful curls.

Jon had decided to play barber.

Jason usually did the shopping alone or we all went together, with people stopping to gawk at our line of well-behaved children. But once we lived close to town and the older kids could watch the babies, he and I could go for groceries by ourselves once in a while. We would always mound our carts full (we usually filled two carts), while other shoppers stared in disbelief as we checked out. On one of our shopping days together, a shift occurred, and I suddenly knew that Jason was angry. I didn't know why, but he spoke in a nasty, abrupt way to the male checker, and his face was hard.

I always felt shaky when he was like that. Whenever we were together in public, I cast my eyes down and tried not to notice anyone, because Jason would watch me to see if I took an interest in other men. So I got used to walking around in a daze, unaware of what was going on around me most of the time. I was so used to it that I did it unconsciously.

On that day, after we finished checking out, we headed through the door, and as soon as we were outside, he exploded.

"I could bust his face in!" he said angrily.

Relieved that it wasn't something I had done, I asked, "What did he do?"

"He was looking at you." He looked sideways at me to see my reaction.

"I hadn't noticed," I replied quietly.

"I know. I watched to see if you were giving him encouragement, but you weren't. I just wanted to bust his damn face in. He had no right looking at my wife that way."

I had given birth to ten children. My hair was scraggly, my shape dumpy, my clothes outdated; I wore knee socks with calf length dresses—yeah, he probably was staring at me and either feeling sorry for me or wondering what the cat drug in.

* * *

In the spring, only a year and a half after we moved to Fuller, Jason was abruptly fired. He came home and said, "Well, it happened sooner than I wanted, and all of my ducky's aren't lined up yet, but I am out of a job." He had been planning to quit anyway, but he wasn't quite ready yet. Jason and Ryan had begun a business for retrofitting classic car parts in the garage, and they had hoped eventually to turn that into a family business.

The firing happened right after Ryan gave his two weeks' notice. He was planning on working full time on the new business that he and his dad had started. The company bought him gifts and gave him a going-away party (he was well liked at the company). The very next day, Jason was suddenly, without notice, escorted to the door. They confiscated his keys, and he was locked out of the building. They were so afraid he would sabotage the company that they didn't want to give him time to do anything. The next day, they allowed him back in under guard to clean out his office. He had worked for them for fourteen years, and they didn't trust him.

Later, when I asked the company president why Jason was fired so I could fill out the unemployment papers, she responded in part,

"Jason thought he and his family members working at Aquatronics ought to be compensated above other employees. He told management he would only give as much effort as he considered adequate for his compensation. At Aquatronics, we expect employees who have agreed to work for a certain amount to give their best efforts. Jason did not want to be a part of the team. He wanted to be the superstar, not subject to the company policies that govern the company. In the end, this made him too difficult to manage."

Jason had assumed he was invaluable. He was fired for arrogance.

Moving West – Jason Gets His Shop

There was dried dog vomit in the closets, mouse feces scattered around, and filth everywhere. The bath and shower showed no sign of use, with spider webs and dust collecting in the corners.

The house was put on the market, and we began to look for a new home. With no idea of which direction to go in, we just picked one. Jason and I had both been brought up on the coast of California. We had been landlocked all those years in Idaho and eastern Washington, so we decided to move west toward the ocean. Jason's prior boss, Darrel, (who helped us when we lived in Remington and had stored our stuff in his garage) quit working for Aquatronics a few years before and moved to a Washington town where he and his wife set up their own veterinarian business. We decided to visit them and check out the vicinity. It was an economically depressed area on the Washington coast.

When I first saw West Harbor, a port town, I was shocked. It was run down, dirty, and decrepit. It was evident that, in the past, it had been a nice place, with beautifully crafted turn-of-the-century homes, old Victorian-style clapboard with gingerbread and other antique architecture. Much of it was in ruin, though, when we visited. We looked farther south and found a small town on the bay called Seaport where we ended up purchasing a piece of land with bay frontage. It was 1.8 acres and had a huge shop on it, so Jason finally got the shop he had always wanted. There was an old, neglected mobile home on the property that was so foul, our eyes watered upon entering. The elderly couple selling it had been brought up during the Depression, and they had hoarded for the fourteen years they lived there. There was dried dog vomit in the closets, mouse feces scattered around, and filth everywhere. The kitchen counters were greasy and had cracked and missing Formica, and the bath and shower showed no signs of use, with cobwebs and dust collecting in the corners. It hadn't been cleaned in a long time—no wonder it made our eyes water!

The shop and all of the outbuildings contained heaped-up boxes and piles of garbage. In moving, the old man took what was valuable to him and left a massive cleanup for us.

The mess was so bad that we had nowhere to sleep the first night we arrived. Early that same morning—after spending days cleaning out our Fuller home, which had been sold—we got into our loaded vehicles and drove for eight hours across Washington to our new home in Seaport. Ryan drove a flatbed truck overloaded with our stuff, and Aleena drove one of the classic cars, while Jason drove the Suburban. Alex stayed behind because he had his own apartment at that point and still worked at Aquatronics.

We made the long trip from eastern to western Washington, and, by the time we arrived, we were exhausted. The children, understandably, were very disappointed with their new home when they arrived and saw what they had to live in—once again. With no place to put our belongings, we began to clean the Seaport place as soon as we arrived. I opened a window in the upper shop and threw things out. Part of this enormous building had rough living quarters where the old man had stayed. His wife had lived in the decayed mobile home. There was a stained mound of carpet that the former owners had rescued from a remodel, planning to have it installed someday. Out it went. The bed that the man had slept in was urine-stained, and the sheets hadn't been washed in years. The bathroom floors reeked of urine and were sticky; someone's aim had been poor. There were so many haphazardly-piled boxes of junk crusted with years of dirt, stacks of wire, pipes, magazines, empty food containers, garage-sale finds, and garbage that it was difficult to navigate.

I desperately hoped that, this time, we would purchase a real home. I even tried to put my foot down. But it didn't happen. We ordered a dumpster, and it took us months to clean up the place. I had the foul carpeting ripped out of the mobile home and new carpeting installed. We painted and wallpapered. But only so much could be done, because Jason said we were going to pull the mobile home off the property and—get this—build our own home—and I still believed him. Not much sense in putting money into a mobile home with water damage, a bad roof, broken, cracked, and stained counters, and holes in the walls, not if a new home would soon be built.

"Soon" never came.

Jason found a job working for a confection processing company in Seattle. It was roughly a three-hour commute. He left early Monday morning with a box of food, enough to last for the week, and came home Thursday evening. He was the engineer in charge of keeping all of the machines running smoothly. His housing was a small abandoned camper parked on the company's property. It was not hooked up to utilities or water; it was just a cold, dark place to sleep. I became certified to homeschool in Washington and continued to homeschool the younger children. The older ones graduated with their GED. I still did not have my driver's license, although I had my learner's permit and was allowed to drive on back roads. Jason would not allow me to drive through an intersection or in town, only on the long stretches along backroads. He still insisted I was incapable of driving and discouraged me. I kept pushing for him to teach me and help me get my license, but after years of being told I couldn't drive, that I would kill the kids, and that women were terrible drivers, I was afraid to drive.

During that summer, Aleena decided to try her hand at baking "real" sourdough bread. I had been brought up in California where I had access to Boudin, San Luis Sourdough, and other West Coast sourdough breads. I often wondered how they baked their breads to get that chewy consistency and crisp crust. Aleena tried for about a month, but she couldn't bake a decent loaf, at least not one she was happy with.

So she issued me this challenge: "No one can bake up real sourdough, Mom. Not *even* you."

That piqued me and started me on my sourdough journey. There are many books, videos, and resources to help new bakers learn to bake sourdough now (including mine). But when I started out, there was very little information available to the general public (My father-in-law actually baked pretty good sourdough and we became sourdough buddies).

After many experiments and failures, I ended up not only baking real sourdough but started a sourdough business, published some bread books, wrote articles, photographed bread, attended baking events, and started teaching baking courses on the Internet. Baking became a large part of my life. This newfound hobby kept me going. I am not sure I could have made it through thirty years without something to relieve the extreme depression and boredom of being stuck in my own home for decades, pregnant, nursing babies, homeschooling, and cleaning a messy house without a reprieve, nothing else to look forward to and no end in sight. Jason hated my involvement in sourdough and accused me of neglecting my household and the kids.

Within three months of our move, Angela, who was then fifteen, underwent emergency surgery for a Meckel's diverticulum, an intussusception of the intestine. This is a rare condition where the Meckel's pouch, a congenital deformity, turns inside the intestine and begins to travel down the digestive tube, drawing the rest of the intestine after itself or turning it inside out. Jason was certain she just had a case of the stomach flu. After we both witnessed her suddenly squirming on the couch and screaming out in pain, she began to vomit continuously. I was troubled about her condition and knew something was seriously wrong.

I argued with him. "There *is* something really wrong with her. We need to take her in to the doctor."

Jason replied, "It's just the flu, she will get over it." After a few days of her condition worsening, I insisted he take her in.

"It's on your shoulders, then," Jason responded to me. "You choose whether she goes in or not."

I knew the game. He expected me to make him feel good and go along with his superior wisdom, but I surprised him. "Okay, then, *take her in.*"

The conversation was ridiculous. Take her in and rule out anything serious or let her die. It was a no-brainer. I didn't see why we had to argue about it. It was just what you do to care for your child.

At the doctor's office, Angela's white blood cell count turned out to be sky high, and so we took her to the emergency room at the nearest hospital. They gave her a CT scan, found a total blockage of the intestine, and then prepped her for emergency surgery. Aleena and I took turns alternately staying with Angela at the hospital and taking care of things at home.

I was alone in the hospital when they performed Angela's surgery. A strange feeling came over me that she would die on the surgery table; emotionally, I was numb. After several hours, when the surgeon came out, he told me that she was okay, but that he had taken out fourteen inches of necrotic intestine—part of her intestines had died—and she was lucky to be alive, as they could have turned gangrenous. I am so glad I insisted that Jason take her to the doctor. Luckily, we were also still covered under Aquatronic's insurance plan.

In the spring of the following year, Benjamin, my very gifted young son who loved to wear floppy hats, play the banjo, and build model boats, had surgery on a bone growth in his upper arm. The tumor was about the size of an egg. We went to Children's Hospital for his surgery. Benjamin was such a trouper. Later in the day, after his surgery, the nurse came in and saw tears rolling down his face. His pain medication had worn off. She asked him what his pain level was between one and ten.

He made her smile when he replied timorously, "Four."

She said to him, "I bet it's more like a nine, and you are just being brave."

It was his turn to smile, as he agreed with her.

Thankfully, there weren't too many medical crises. With eleven in the family and me pregnant for so many years, we were pretty lucky.

FALL 2005: I GO HOME!

It was surreal for me as we approached our destination.
I hadn't seen my childhood home in decades.

LATER IN THE FALL OF 2005, my parents celebrated their fiftieth wedding anniversary. The family put a lot of effort into getting everyone to make it to the celebration. I had not been back to see my family for decades. My parents were hoping that all twelve of their children would be able to attend. They were pretty successful in their efforts, as only one of my siblings couldn't make it. Matching T-shirts were made up for all twelve of us, and we had a big celebration at the church hall. Jason relented to my entreaties to go, and we packed most of the children into the Suburban and made the twenty-one-hour trip down the coast. It was surreal for me, as we approached our destination.

I hadn't seen my childhood home in over twenty years.

Before we left, I purchased a dress on eBay to wear to the wedding, and I lost some weight. I also asked Aleena to trim my hair for the wedding. It was long, straight, and straggly looking, and I was embarrassed by it. She asked Jason if she could, and, for the first time ever, he gave permission. When she trimmed my hair, something strange happened—it started to curl underneath, near the back of my neck. Aleena had trimmed it a little shorter than she should have, so we told Jason it just looked shorter because it was finally all even.

As we neared the area of California where we had grown up, I didn't recognize much of it. Hilly farmlands once covered in oaks were now covered in expensive houses. It's weird how expansive the memories of old building and places can be, only to shrink in size when seen through the lens of reality. I had assumed I would never see my home again, since Jason wouldn't allow me to go anywhere by myself, and he didn't like me to be around my family. For the first time, I met nieces and nephews that I had never seen. They were children of my brothers and sisters who had grown up together but had never met us, although some of them had visited us in Idaho or Washington.

Our children were a bit overwhelmed when they suddenly met my eleven siblings and Jason's six siblings. My parents had fifty-four grandchildren, and Jason's parents had twenty grandchildren. So our children had lots of cousins! Jason felt proud of himself for "allowing" me to go to a ladies-only luncheon that my sister hosted. I could tell he was nervous, though, and worried about the "bad influence" my family would have on me and the children. He needed to feel he was in control.

Jason took us on a memory-lane trip to the area where he had grown up, seven miles to the south of my parents' home. He showed the children some of the houses he'd built in the avocado orchards and where some of his family members lived. He didn't particularly want to see his siblings, but he reluctantly attended a barbeque given in our honor by one of his older sisters. He was uncomfortable visiting with his family members and commented that he never needed to see them again.

My children later expressed surprise that the Reys side of the family were so nice, loving, and affectionate. Sure, they had met a few of the relatives over the years when they had come to visit us in the northwest but had heard their whole lives that the Reys family was a bad influence, that they were corrupted Catholics who were not to be trusted. It felt so good to be around my family again, to belong and feel like one of them. It had been a long time since I had felt wanted, loved, and cared about without conditions. Perhaps my brainwashing loosened on that visit, as I began to remember what life was like in the real world. That was exactly why Jason had kept me away from them for so long, and why he was so worried about their influence during our visit.

CHAPTER 6: WEDDINGS

Who wants to be part of a religion or belief system where rules, unkindness, and superiority take the place of love?

Two years after our move, Alex was dismissed from his job at Aquatronics, lost his apartment, and became homeless. When I found out, I invited him to move back in with us. He went from a nice bachelor apartment to a platform he built in the rafters of our unheated garage. It was only large enough for a sleeping bag, and he accessed it by climbing on top of the car underneath the platform. Unfortunately, he was used to this kind of suffering from his childhood, but it must have been harder after having had his own nice place for a while. He got a job working at a nearby shipyard where Ryan and Brent had also found work. There he met a lovely girl who became his wife and the mother of my first grandchild.

In the spring, Alex and his girlfriend found out they were expecting a baby, so they got married outside of the Catholic Church. For upstanding, judgmental Catholics like us, it was devastating, and we did not attend the wedding. It would have meant giving our blessing to his breach of faith. Our oldest son Ryan was the only one with enough love in his heart to try and attend Alex's wedding, but he drove around and could not find the church. Secretly, I was proud of Ryan for bucking the belief system that had been shoved down his throat for years. Letting go of love for the sake of religion is tantamount to throwing the baby out with the bathwater. Who wants to be part of a religion or belief system where rules, unkindness, and superiority take the place of love? I had been brainwashed by this thinking, as well, and felt it was wrong to attend his wedding.

In June, Aleena was married. Hers was the first Catholic wedding in the family. She was a radiantly beautiful bride. Angela, who was the cake queen, baked and decorated a beautiful banana cake for her sister's wedding reception.

It was a surreal time for me. I couldn't believe one of my babies was getting married. Several of my family members made the long trip north to attend the wedding—my brother, Tony, and his large family of eleven children, together with my mother, one of my sisters, Marie, her kids, and Jason's parents all came. During the reception, one of the tables broke and food flew all over the floor, and then my mom, who had traveled two days with the family caravan to attend the wedding, had to be rushed to the hospital.

She had congestive heart failure, and the lining around her lungs had filled with almost a liter and a half of liquid, which pressed on her lungs making it hard for her to breathe. I spent the rest of the afternoon in the hospital with her. One of my sisters took me in her car and we stayed with mom. So I missed Aleena's wedding reception. I had to witness my mom undergoing the treatment to draw the fluid from around her lungs. Without any anesthesia, they plunged a long needle into her back and withdrew the fluid. I hope my mom never has to suffer so much pain again (she did have more suffering to undergo and died in the spring of 2015).

When we brought Mom back to our place, my siblings and I had a conference on what we should do. Mom needed to get home right away, and the two-day trip packed in a car with a bunch of kids would be too much for her. We all decided I should be the one to fly with our mother, and then I could return on another flight. Since my siblings had brought their children and still needed to make the long trek back, I was really the only one who could attend to her on the flight home. I had older children who could watch my younger ones, and Jason would be near enough, if there were any problems.

But then, Jason flew into a rage. He stood out in the middle of the yard, and, with his parents and my family members watching, he burst into a tirade about how I was not going to take off by myself and how *he* would make the decision on what was to be done with my mom. Jason's father and mother stared at him in disbelief. They had never seen him treat me this way or be so unreasonable and rude. He had always been so careful to maintain his façade around others.

Jason's father said, "Why not just let her go with her mom? You are being unreasonable."

I thought Jason's mom would be upset with me, but instead, Mrs. Gannon turned to her husband and began to berate him loudly. "This is how you always treat me," she yelled at him. "Now you can see what you are like."

Jason's father looked embarrassed and stared at the ground.

Jason asserted himself. "I will take her home. No need for anyone to fly."

I replied, "It is two days in a car. She would probably be more comfortable if she flew home in a couple of hours instead of spending the twenty-plus-hour drive in a hot car." (The air conditioning in our vehicle didn't work.)

I was beside myself with amazement and consternation. Jason looked like a madman. He was enraged and wanted to have control

of the situation. Family members surrounded us in a circle, staring at us in surprise. My brother, Tony, called a truce and said he
wanted to take me out for a walk so everyone could cool down.

So we went for a walk. This brother, the one born right after me,
was my confidant. Over the years, when I had a chance to talk to
someone, it was him.

"He needs to be in control, Tessy," Tony said carefully.

"I know, but it makes me so mad. It's Mom we should be concerned about, not him. He is self-absorbed, insecure, and doesn't
want me out of his sight. He feels he has to call the shots because we
all got together and decided what to do for Mom without his input."

We both decided it would be best for Jason to make the decision,
instead of allowing the whole thing to blow out of proportion.

So Jason and I took my mother home. About halfway, the trans-
mission gasket blew, so we hobbled the car to the nearest town, got
a motel room, and took the car to a local garage to be fixed. We
told them about our emergency trip, so they expedited the repairs.
We got the cheapest motel we could in town. The blankets were
old, rough, and felt dirty. There were two double beds in a small
room with maybe eighteen inches of space between our bed and my
mother's. That night, Jason insisted we have sex.

"Yeah, right," I replied. "And if that was your mom in the bed
next to us, would you be asking that?"

"No, I guess not." He rolled over and went to sleep.

We got her home the following evening, after two very long days
in the car. It was much harder on her than a plane flight would have
been, but at least Jason was back in the driver's seat.

*   *   *

Joseph was a bicycle enthusiast, and he encouraged me to take
up biking. I had not ridden since I was a kid, and it sounded like
fun, so I asked Jason if I could. He thought it would be a good idea
for me to get out and get some exercise, so he found me a bike at

the church rummage sale and brought it home. He himself had a neglected touring bike that he'd bought early in our marriage. Since I was going to start riding, he felt he had to, too. However, his and Joseph's bikes were of good quality, while mine was a three-speed, heavy and hard to ride. The first time I got on it, I rode down the street a short way, and my legs quickly began to hurt, so I turned around, but could not make it back up the driveway!

My son encouraged me and said, "Mom, just ride a little each day, and it will be easier soon."

So I did, and when we all rode together, I had to pump continuously without a rest because of the gearing. I couldn't keep up with them and felt like a failure, so I started to ride by myself. I told Jason I needed a pair of pants to ride in, and he got upset about that—and insisted that I wear a dress while biking.

"That's why the bar goes down for a girl's bike, so they can wear a dress," he stated triumphantly.

I tried to bike while wearing a dress, but it kept flying up in my face and showing the world my underwear and slip. *That's real modest,* I thought to myself. So I snuck out one day with my friend who drove me to town, and I bought a pair of pants. I knew inside that he had no right to tell me that I couldn't wear pants. That was not respecting or honoring your partner; it was just making my life hard because *he* was insecure.

Jason was upset when he saw what I had done, but he relented, saying, "You can wear pants when you are riding, but you *have* to take them off when you get home."

"You try riding a bike with a dress on," I replied. "I'm pretty sure it won't be a minute until you realize how ridiculous it is." My attitude appeared to have scared him, and he became more insecure. I wasn't willing to be a doormat anymore.

Eventually, I bought a nice bicycle and had it sent to the house through the mail. Since I had struggled with the more difficult bike, I didn't realize it but had built up stronger muscles. When I got on my new one, after Joseph assembled it, I flew! I loved it! I loved the feeling of freedom when I flew down the road with the wind against my face.

*   *   *

In the fall, after working for two years at the candy factory, Jason was fired for arrogance again. They got tired of him telling them how to run their company and making snide remarks to the people in charge. While his job lasted, though, he brought home fifty-pound boxes of discarded chocolates, and we were the favorite stopping place for neighbors and friends.

In October, I held my first grandson in my arms. I was in the hospital room as he was born, and I filmed his first moments. Alex was now a proud daddy, and I was amazed, wondering how many grandchildren I would hold in my arms eventually.

When he became unemployed, Jason threw himself into making a go of his business with Ryan. They ordered machining stock and drew up CAD plans for adaptors for classic car parts. Jason took care of the machining end of things, while Ryan took care of the sales and paperwork part of the business. The relationship between Jason and his older children was an uneasy one. The older children wanted and needed their independence, but Jason seemed to put a roadblock in their way. He demanded rent from any of the children who were working, and then made it impossible for them to leave. The children were paying the bills with the rent, and so he needed them to stay.

Jason loved them in his own way, as much as he was capable, and tried to spend time with them when he became unemployed. We could pick a lot of blueberries or blackberries when we worked together. Whenever the whole family went to harvest our quota of clams, we came home with a large haul—at ten to twenty clams each, depending upon the type, and eleven people, that was a lot of clams. Jason took the boys fishing for salmon, tuna, and sturgeon in season, hunting for deer in the fall and Chanterelle mushroom gathering along the slopes when it began to get cold. On Fridays, the family would sit together watching old movies or around a fire pit, the men drinking home-brewed beer and smoking cigars and, at times, playing musical instruments.

RYAN LEAVES HOME

My heart broke. I hugged him goodbye and knew I would miss him terribly, but I was also happy that he was strong enough to go against the control of his father and be free!

RYAN HAD BEEN WORKING AS A MECHANIC for two years but had become frustrated with life. As the summer wore on, he continued to work on the side, taking care of customers for the home business he shared with Jason. At some point, Jason lost interest in the business and stopped machining. The machining stock lay on the garage floor, neglected. The customers had to be paid back after delays, which lasted months.

Years earlier, when Ryan wanted to go to college, Jason had promised him that, if he stayed home and helped with the business instead of going to college, Jason would cover most of his expenses, and they would get rich together. Ryan had kept up his side of the bargain. He had also sunk a lot of money into the business and paid his dad rent for a bedroom, even though Jason was supposed to cover his expenses. We didn't realize then that Jason was a compulsive liar. With Jason's apparent lack of interest in filling orders, Ryan got fed up. He felt like his life was going nowhere and his opportunities were fading. One day, in September of 2008, he pulled in a trailer, filled it up with his stuff, and left for Texas. My heart broke. I hugged him goodbye and knew I would miss him terribly, but I was also happy that he was strong enough to go against the control of his father and be free! He was twenty-seven, and it was long past due.

After several months of unemployment, with me filling out the paperwork and applying for jobs for him online, Jason got a job at a security business in Tulia, Washington. The commute wasn't as far as before, and he decided to get a motel room instead of living at work during the work week. Jason was well liked at this business, and he seemed to enjoy the job. He worked on security mechanisms and plastic molding machines.

A few times, when Jason came home on the weekend, I was on my period. It was inevitable and beyond my control. After one such incidence, he had a fit of anger, wouldn't talk to me, and sulked. I didn't realize he was upset about me being unavailable.

Then he blurted out, "You deliberately had your period on the weekend so I couldn't have sex." He went on to blame me and said it was my fault. Then he got so mad, he went and sat outside on a bench all day long and wouldn't talk to anyone. His face was like a mask, immobile, dark with rage. The children asked me what was wrong with their dad.

I answered them, "Go ask him."(Years later, I found out that one son did go ask him and because of the answer he received, began to suspect his dad was crazy.)

After that accusation, I felt that there was something really wrong with my husband.

Mom's Surgery

I thought it would be nice to be myself for once while I was away from him. It felt amazing to be all alone, by myself, acting like a real adult, without anyone spying on me.

In the fall of 2007, my mom had to have heart surgery. None of my other siblings were available at the time, so I asked Jason if I could go help my mom. He never let me go home or anywhere else by myself for almost the whole of our marriage. He was pretty stressed and didn't want me to go, but he relented.

I was shocked and thrilled to be able to go home by myself for the first time since my marriage. On the trip, I wore a dress, but took—snuck—some pants and a T-shirt (my riding clothes) to wear

at my parents' house. It was amazing, when you think about it—
having to sneak clothes. I thought it would be nice to be myself
for once, while I was away from him. It felt wonderful to be all
alone, acting like a real adult without anyone spying on me. While
on the plane, another passenger asked if I was a Mormon. With my
outdated, calf-length corduroy dress and knee socks, I looked out
of place.

It was a ten-day trip, and by the seventh day, Jason was furious.
He felt that I had not contacted him often enough. Besides caring for
my mother in the hospital and at home after her surgery, I was also
having fun with my family. I wore pants and went out to lunch with
one of my sisters whom he despised and wanted me to have nothing
to do with. She had accused him of inappropriate behavior during
the time when Jason and I were courting. Somehow either he found
out—was spying on me again—or assumed that I was having fun,
and it annoyed him.

I was so amazed that I could be and feel like a normal person
when I was around my original family. They loved me and let me
be me. I felt accepted, and I liked myself when I was with them. The
contrast was startling, compared to the treatment I received at home.
It had been decades since I felt like a real person with a right to think
my own thoughts and make my own decisions. The fear and stress
were gone when I was with my family.

I flew home, but it was so hard to get on that plane. If I didn't
have children to go home to, I never would have gotten on that
plane. He was so enraged when I arrived, that I was scared to walk
off that plane. When I saw his face at the airport, I knew he would
have killed me if he could have. His face looked stone-hard and
blanched; his eyes glittered with hatred. He let me have it on the
way home. He lit into me for all he was worth and said lots of
untrue terrible things, berating me, calling me names and tearing
me to shreds. He hated that I had a good time. I don't know how
he found out I was wearing pants or having lunch with my sister.
Later, in the dregs of the evening, he asked me for a divorce. I
felt a thrill in my heart but quickly squelched it. He was playing a

game. He didn't want a divorce; he was baiting me to see if I did. I told him I felt that even if we had to live in separate rooms, the children didn't need us to divorce. I regret that I didn't confront him and say yes to a divorce right then; it might have saved a lot of heartache later.

I was exhausted, drained trying to be someone I wasn't, and sick of following rules that made no sense. I had tired of the games, the twisted logic, the walking on eggshells, the brainwashing, trying to figure out how to keep him happy so he would leave us all alone. Some part of me wanted to reclaim my lost self, but I was still afraid of Jason and what he might do. It was as if two people inside of me fought against each other—the one who wanted to be free and the one who was desperately afraid.

The one who wanted to be free had a milestone victory in the summer of 2008. After having a learner's permit renewed for over ten years (*Yeah, really! Can you believe it?*), I finally got my license to drive a car.

It astonished me that I ever accomplished this milestone after the years of mental abuse over it. The feeling of elation after passing the test was unforgettable. However, I was still afraid to drive even a mile down the road. With my determination and insistence, Jason bought me a used car, and I drove it around our small town, doing a few errands once in a while.

I had to work up my courage every time I got into my car, though. It didn't help my nerves that, the day after he bought the car, I drove it two miles down the road—with him supervising—and then, while turning into a parking lot, my foot hit the gas instead of the brakes. I gunned the engine and smashed into the side of a local business. The bags deployed, we got hit in the face, and our ears rang.

After that, Jason didn't like me driving, especially when he was gone to work during the week. So one day he started using my car as his commuter car, after he repaired the damage to the front end and fixed the building I hit.

I was humiliated and horrified by what had happened and didn't drive for about six months afterward. Then, some of my family and friends, knowing what had happened, began telling me stories of how they had also gunned the engine and stepped on the gas instead of the brakes or had hit posts, backed up when they should have gone forward, and other confessions of an average driver (even seasoned drivers have mishaps). I began to feel better, especially when I remembered that Jason and some of my sons had similar incidents with their cars.

At that point, I was forty-nine and never thought I would do it, but I finally got my driver's license. Getting my license gave me back a little of my self-esteem and self-confidence, but it was just the start. I was finally becoming an adult. It was about time!

Brent's Breakdown

> *Brent was surrounded by police, and as he got out of the vehicle, he screamed at them, "Shoot me."*

Ryan, Aleena, and Alex had all left home. Brent decided that it was time for him to leave. As a small child, he had taught himself to program and quickly passed up the other kids. I encouraged my children to use computers. They had some restrictions, but I felt that computers were the future. Many homeschooling parents at the time had restricted their children from computers and technology until they were older, believing it interfered with their development. I felt it would be the same as not letting them read until they were older... a loss of precious learning time. We also had some Internet classes as part of our homeschooling. So, eventually, most of the children had their own computers. They were assembled by hand from reused discards, hand-me-downs, or garage-sale finds.

Brent and his father locked horns over computer usage. Jason didn't even want the kids to be on the computers; he felt they were a waste of time. It's doubtful he would have been hired on as an engineer without being computer savvy, though. I think sometimes it was hard for Jason—in his mind, he still straddled the fence of being a mountain man from two hundred years ago, yet was intelligent and curious enough to want to learn about all of the new technology.

Brent was the dreamer: sensitive, caring, and smart.

He loaded up his vehicle one day and set out for California, where my original family lived. He was welcomed into my brother, Tony's, home. My brother had eleven children, and most of them were still at home. Brent found a job working with an aircraft design company and became fast friends with one of his girl cousins. He seemed happy at first, but as time went by, I began to receive disturbing letters from him and then scary phone calls. He was overwhelmed with feelings and strange thoughts, and felt his mind was on fire. Twice, he called and told me he had suicidal thoughts. He got his own apartment to get away from the chaos of living with my brother's large family, but his meltdown continued.

I didn't know what was going on. None of us did. In retrospect, it all makes sense, but at the time it was bewildering, scary, and a terrible experience for everyone involved. I asked him to see a doctor, and he replied that he had seen a doctor and was prescribed Zoloft. However, his symptoms worsened, and he began to have total meltdowns.

One day, I got a call from law enforcement. They had been called in to look for Brent. He had left a cryptic message at work after giving away all of his tools.

"Does he have a gun?" the police wanted to know.

I knew that he did, so I told them yes. They informed me that they had searched Brent's room and found a suicide note but no sign of a gun. Then I was really disturbed and called my parents, who lived in the area. But no one had seen him.

It turned out that he had taken the whole bottle of Zoloft in an attempt to kill himself, and then went berserk. He went on a rampage, looking for his girl cousin who hid out in her uncle's house.

Eventually, the police surrounded Brent, and, as he got out of the vehicle, he screamed at them, "Shoot me."

He was trying to commit suicide by police. They took him to the emergency room, where he was given something to counteract the medication, and then to jail for his own safety. He was put under observation and given counseling. He hated being in jail and asked my dad to bail him out. But Brent's instability convinced my dad that his grandson would be safer getting help where he was.

My dad was the only one in my extended family who visited him while he was in jail. It was a terrible time in Brent's life, as his world fell apart around him and everyone he loved abandoned him. They were all scared; they didn't know what was going on.

After Brent was evaluated, he was put on medication for bipolar disorder. What he was going through was a cascading bipolar event. The doctor he had seen earlier for help did not take a family history, or he would have found out that OCD, epilepsy, depression, and bipolar were part of his family history. He had been prescribed the worst thing a person suffering from bipolar could take—Zoloft—and it made him violent. Brent was told he could sue the doctor for malpractice, but he told me he did not want to pursue that avenue.

Broken, without hope, and feeling like his family and friends had deserted him, Brent came home looking for support. He did not find it. Jason told him harshly that he was not allowed home, as he didn't want Brent around the children, since he said Brent couldn't be trusted. Rejected again, Brent went and stayed with Alex, his wife, and their new baby. Alex welcomed him with open arms.

Things did not improve for Brent, though. His mental breakdown continued, because he did not get follow-up medical help and didn't really know what was going on in his own mind. One day, I received a call from him. He seemed emotionally detached. He said he loved me. When he said goodbye, it seemed as if he meant forever.

A terrible feeling of dread washed over me. I called Alex immediately and said, "Drop whatever you are doing and drive to your house as fast as you can. I have a bad feeling that Brent is going to do something desperate."

Later, Alex called me back and sounded upset, but he said, "Everything is okay, Mom. I got here in time."

It wasn't until a few years later, when Brent gave a talk at a suicide prevention gathering, that I heard the story from his own mouth of what had happened that day. In horror, I listened as my son told the audience how broken he had been, and how his own family rejected him when he needed them the most. He went on to tell them how he had finally reached a point where he could not go on. He had retreated to a special place on Alex's property with a loaded gun, had cocked the trigger, and had his finger on it. Then he made a pact with God. With his heart torn out and his world completely dark, he told God that if someone didn't walk over the hill in the next five minutes, he would pull the trigger and end his suffering. With one minute to spare, Alex crested the hill and saw his brother with a gun pointed toward his own chest, his finger on the trigger, and tears streaming down his face.

Brent finally got help and the medication he needed for his bipolar disorder. I don't like to think of what Alex would have found if he had arrived one minute later or hadn't sped the whole way home or didn't find where his brother had gone to on his property or if I hadn't listened to my instincts that told me something was terribly wrong. It still feels like a close call whenever I remember that day.

CHAPTER 7:
BEAUTIFUL HAWAII

And then, I heard a still, small voice inside me. "You have the key in your own hand, and you always have."

JASON CONTINUED TO COMMUTE TO TULIA, but the policies that the new United States president put into place caused his company to relocate to Mexico. Jason was asked to move to Mexico, too, and continue working for the company. However, another job offer came in at the same time. We were offered a position, as a family, to oversee two macadamia nut farms on the Big Island of Hawaii. In Fuller, Jason made $80,000 per year. In Tulia, he made $65,000 per year as an engineer. In Hawaii, we would be lucky to make $12,000 per year, but the housing, gas, utilities, car insurance, cars, and much of the food (fruits, wild pig meat, and, of course, mac nuts!) would be free. Plus, it was *Hawaii*. Who could pass up a chance to live in Hawaii at least once in their lifetime?

We weren't sure we could manage it financially, but we decided to give it a try, at least for the adventure of it. We entered into long email and phone discussions with Dr. Mitch and his wife, Tanya, who owned three Hawaiian farms on the Big Island. We would be managing two of the farms; the other was managed by the grandparents of friends of ours, Barry and Shayla. Dr. Mitch and Tanya lived in Alaska, where his medical practice was located, but they spent a lot of time in Hawaii and had invested in property on the island.

The two Hawaiian farms we were going to manage were being taken care of by an older bachelor who was dying of cancer, and, due to his condition, he planned to fly back to the mainland to be with his family. Since the doctor needed someone to take his place right away, Joseph flew to Hawaii to care for the farms until we arrived; we had a wedding to attend.

Angela had met her soon-to-be husband on Catholic Match, an internet dating site, and they were getting married in June. They moved the wedding date up just so we could attend before flying off to start our new life. We made the long trip to Arizona by car to be present at the ceremony. It is incredibly hot in Arizona in the summer. While there, we took the youngest children to visit the zoo. Being the greenhorns that we were, we neglected to bring water, and it was 108 degrees in the early morning. The animals looked miserable in the heat. Water-misting areas were nicely provided along the footpaths. But there were very few places to get drinking water, because the zoo sold bottled water and wanted visitors to purchase it.

The wedding went well. Aleena had flown in to be the bridesmaid and was very pregnant with her first baby. It was a beautiful ceremony, and the couple was ecstatically in love. But I remember it with a tinge of sadness. I felt left out of the celebration—I wasn't invited to the bridal shower and had no part in the wedding or preparation, we were just onlookers. It didn't even feel like I was the mother of the bride. I tried to set aside my feelings, because I knew how terrible the pressure could be during a wedding and I was happy my daughter had found a man who really seemed to love her.

The groom's family hired a DJ, and the music was great for reception dancing. I really wanted to dance, but I knew Jason did not want me to, and he certainly wasn't going to. We sat way back in the furthest corner, away from the activity. We must have seemed odd to everyone. When it came time for the father-bride dance, our sweet, beautiful bride Angela came over to her father, her face lit with hopeful expectation, but Jason declined her vehemently. He was not going to dance, period. I wanted to get up and dance with her, wanted to so badly, but I couldn't. I was frozen to my seat, still lacking the courage to stand on my own yet. Angela's face fell with disappointment; her eyes looked down in embarrassment. How awkward and sad for a father to refuse to dance with his daughter at her wedding, with all of her new in-laws around to witness the rejection.

Thankfully, Benjamin came and grabbed his sister and danced with her in place of her father. Everyone present danced and had fun, except the two oddballs in the corner. The bride, my daughter, was the best dancer on the floor; she boogied in her wedding dress. I'd missed out on the reception at Aleena's wedding because my mom had gotten sick, and now, at Angela's reception, instead of joy, I felt out of place, angry with myself, and sad. There was no one to blame but myself. If I had gotten up and danced the night away, it would have been too bad whatever Jason might have thought or done.

Today, I go back in my memory and dance at Angela's wedding. I take her in my arms after her dad rejects her, and we dance together. Instead of the terrible look of disappointment and shame, her face lights up with a radiant glow. I smile back with joy and love. It is the only way to replace the part of my heart that was ripped out by my own lack of courage on that most special day of her life.

Joseph missed the wedding because he went to Hawaii in our place to take over management of the Hawaii farms until we could arrive. Angela and her new husband went to Hawaii on their honeymoon, however, and stopped to visit her brother while they were there. So really, Angela and Joseph were in Hawaii before we ever set foot on the volcano island.

*   *   *

We circled over the islands before we landed, and my heart jumped at how beautiful and exotic it looked from the air. We brought ten fifty-pound suitcases and nine carry-on bags full of clothes, kitchenware, and tools to begin our new life. We flew to Hawaii on the very last day of June 2009, and there began the last nine months of our marriage.

My first breath of air in Hawaii was warm, humid, and smelled like flowers. Hawaii was a magical place for me: the sights, sounds, and smells were lovely, soothing, and peaceful. The culture was laidback and easy-going. Things got done eventually; it was called, "Island time." It's no place for an A-type personality. You could wear or not wear whatever you wanted, and no one paid any attention. The area around Lanoa, the closest town to where we lived, was a refuge for those who enjoy the hippie and communal lifestyle.

We drove to the smallest of the farms; it had thirteen fenced-in acres of macadamia nut trees. The dwelling where we were going to live was not really a house but a shed, with part of it converted to living quarters. Outside in front was where the equipment for processing and sorting macadamia nuts was kept.

There was a large water tank called a catchment for storing rain runoff from the roof. Most people on the Big Island used some type of catchment system for their water needs. We also had solar and propane and we were off grid. I brought most of what I needed to continue my sourdough business. I sold sourdough starters but found it was too difficult to process and store the starters in a humid environment without benefit of adequate refrigeration, so I transferred my business to Ryan in Texas. He was out of a job and needed to make house payments. Our only means of an internet connection, at first, was at an internet café. Later, we set up a satellite connection and a printer where we lived.

There was a lot of poverty amid large, rich homes in Hawaii. The underground word was that the main crop supporting the residents was marijuana, although it was illegal. We were warned not to go walking anywhere on the desolate back roads, as we could potentially run into someone's illegal operation and be at risk of getting shot.

What I found, however, was that with some precautions, Hawaii was like everywhere else: there were mostly nice people with kind hearts and a few nasty people who tried to ruin life for everyone else. Actually, Hawaii seemed to me to have an unusually large amount of kind-hearted, welcoming people. They do try to live by their spirit of *aloha,* and they teach their children to respect others. I felt very welcomed by the people I met there.

During our first week, we cleaned the living quarters, and then went to Hilo for supplies like pillows and bulk food. We also picked up propane to run the oven, refrigerator, and hot-water tank.

We toured the three farms, two of which we would manage, and met Shayla and Barry, who managed the third farm. Shayla and Barry later became family when their granddaughter, Cherise, married our son, Brent. The farm where we lived had thirteen acres of macadamia nut trees and was totally fenced in and locked. The second farm of around twenty-three acres was a bit of a drive toward Lanoa. It was neglected and had mac nut trees, noni plants, longans, guavas, avocados, and a hairy, funny-looking red fruit called rambutans. I didn't like longans when I first tried them, but there were a few varieties, and when I tried a second variety, I thought they were pretty good; eventually, I became addicted to them like everyone else. Longans look like a large tan-colored marble, and when you open them, inside is a white-ish, translucent, fleshy ball, much like an eyeball.

The second farm needed a lot of attention, as it had serious problems of neglect, some plant disease, and damage from wild pigs.

The wild pigs were a serious problem in some areas of Hawaii. They rooted up and ravaged the farms, and they could be menacing if you met them in person, especially the large male boars with huge, scary teeth. We often saw pigs on the back roads early in the morning or in the evening. We were expected to kill as many wild pigs as we could, to control the damage done to the farms. Pigs that feasted on wild fruit, avocados, and mac nuts produced very tasty pork—although I don't care for pork. Their jaws and teeth were amazing—you could hear them crunching the nuts from a distance.

*   *   *

All of the doctor's farms plus his vacation house were located in the Launea region on the Big Island of Hawaii.

The third farm, managed by Shayla and Barry, was in Kalaa and was about thirty acres. The farm they managed contained a large collection of exotic fruits and trees from all over the world. The doctor and his wife had been collecting the plants for years. We were allowed to eat any of the produce from all three farms, and so were Barry and Shayla.

The first day after we arrived, we drove the loop around the southeastern part of the island.

When we reached Kalapana, we stopped and got out to see where the lava crawled over the road. We could also see the billowing plume of steam in the distance where the molten lava poured into the sea. Then, as we headed northeast toward Kapoho, we followed the coast and took in some really beautiful scenery, with drop-off cliffs and jagged lavascapes lined with lush, overhanging trees and palms. The varying ocean hues of deep indigo to aqua were intensely beautiful.

Kapoho is a place of whispering past moments lost forever. It was a settlement covered over by lava in the 1960s. A person can almost imagine the meandering houses dotted along the coast and the children riding their bikes… all gone now. One of the things that astonished me the most about Hawaii was how very little soil it had.

It is all lava, at least in the southern part where the land is newborn.
Yet the plants will grow right out of the lava rock, their roots gnarled
and twined throughout the craggy rock. Planting something meant
taking a pickaxe to the ground.

A week later, on July 6th, we drove the whole perimeter of the Big
Island. The drive itself was about six-and-a-half hours, not including
stops. I took videos and pictures along the way. It was sort of an
overview trip, to get an idea of what Hawaii was like. For a first-time
visitor, it could be a bit shocking, not only because of the beauty, but
because of the diversity. The different regions of Hawaii range from
barren volcanic desert to highlands of eucalyptus trees reminiscent
of California to verdant green pastures and exotic jungles dotted
with waterfalls. There are an amazing variety of seascapes, from
white ground coral sand beaches and black, green, and grey sands
to rough, overhanging cliff beaches and rocky beaches that contain
some of the most incredible underwaterscapes I have ever seen. We
saw acres of macadamia nuts and coffee plantations as we headed
south along the western coast.

In the middle of July, we visited the Kapoho Thermal Hot Pond.
It is a large, man-made outdoor pool intermixed with the natural
setting of the ocean. Volcanic hot water runs into the pool on one
end, and the ocean water crashes in from the opposite side, mixing

the hot and cold water. It is ringed with coconut trees and has a park on one side. The water temperature varies, depending upon the tide. We met up with Doctor Mitch and his wife Tanya for a picnic and to go swimming. Barry and Shayla were also invited. The day was warm and sunny, and we had a wonderful time. Hamburgers were slapped on the outdoor grill and lemonade was passed around. I brought some homemade Poquito Beans and sourdough banana bread. We arrived at 11:00 a.m. and stayed until 4:00 p.m. By 1:00 p.m., I noticed that my shoulders felt hot, so I tried to make sure the children and I stayed under some shade. We didn't realize that the sun so close to the tropics was a different beast than the one in Washington—or even in California, where I had grown up.

By nightfall, as the sunburn set in, Jon, Misha, and I were in misery. We were badly burned. Our fiery red shoulders were studded with a multitude of deep-pocketed blisters. Poor Jon, who is a ginger, had not exposed his pasty-white skin to the sun for years and was in extreme pain. I laid wet, cold cloths on their hot skin and used aloe vera to soothe the pain. I could not lie on my sides, because the pain was too intense, so I slept on my back; if I didn't move an inch, I could bear it—almost. Jason bounced into bed, causing me anguish, which I complained about.

He, of course, wanted to romp.

"It's just sunburn," he said. "I've got one, too, and it isn't that bad."

"Even when you move on the bed, it causes me a lot of pain," I replied.

"Well, you can just lay there and not do anything."

I was so angry inside. I knew he wouldn't care and expected it.

"No, it hurts way too much." I was going out on a limb, because the rules were that I was never allowed to say no. But I was in severe pain.

Annoyed, he flopped down on his side of the bed and proceeded to bounce around the rest of the night whenever he needed to shift. I am sure my mind over-exaggerated how much he moved, but even when I breathed, it hurt. I was not allowed to sleep on the couch or anywhere else except the marriage bed whenever he was at home. If he was infuriated, *he* could choose to go and sleep on the couch; I wished that he had. Our sunburns healed, but I paid more attention to our amount of sun exposure after that, making sure to bring plenty of water to drink everywhere we went and bringing a large tube of sunscreen.

*   *   *

We threw ourselves into island life. Dr. Mitch and Tanya showed us how to run a macadamia nut farm. We learned about the picking, sorting, and care of mac nuts, where to find the wild pigs, and the locations of the abundant avocados, guavas, papayas, and other exotic fruits too numerous to mention. Some of the fruit we sold or traded—the longans seemed to be a favorite amongst the locals; we also bought other fruits and vegetables at the local farmers' markets in Lanoa and Hilo. One of our favorites was the rare white pineapple; its sweetness and flavor was unparalleled. I enjoyed the ping-pong bananas because of how adorable they looked, and another exotic fruit, breadfruit, that could be cooked up various ways, either sweet or savory. Once, when Joseph, Benjamin, and I were walking along a back road, we spied some pink bananas. I never even imagined there were pink bananas!

I collected Hawaiian and Indian skirts and dresses. I loved the large batik rayon shawls; they were multi-purposed for a hot climate. A shawl could be held over the head for shade or soaked in water and then draped over the shoulders to keep one cool through evaporation. They tied up nicely, depending on their size, for a beach cover-up or exotic skirt. The brightly colored cloth could be spread out on the sand to sit on for a picnic or to lounge on for tanning. I also rolled them up in the window to make shade in a hot car.

During the rest of the summer, we visited the Kiluea Caldera at Volcano Park and walked through a volcano tube, the Chain of Craters Road, where we saw the two kinds of lava: the rough lava, called 'a'ā lava; and smooth lava, called pahhoho. We hiked out to see the petroglyphs while we were there, visited Akaka Falls, and took a drive down Government Beach Road, following the southeastern coast of the Big Island. That is the area people call, "The place that time forgot." It is remote and overgrown with exotic jungle plants and trees; it has the feel of being very ancient. We stopped at the lighthouse on Cape Kumukahi at the end of Highway 132, where NOAA monitors world air quality.

As summer wore on, we spent more time gathering and sorting macadamia nuts. The doctor employed several locals to work gathering nuts, and the fastest nut picker was a sixty-five-year-old Filipino woman. You could learn a lot by watching her, but she didn't like to be watched. It was hard on the legs and back to crouch for long hours and gather the nuts into bags. The bags weighed around sixty-plus pounds and had to be brought in at the end of the day. The nuts were then loaded into a machine that tore off the hulls and spit the nuts out into a holding area where they were sorted as they rolled down into the air-drying bins. Every single nut had to be looked at as it rolled by, so that the bug-infested, rotten, or moldy nuts could be picked out and used as fuel, sold at discount, or traded to those who wanted to pick through them. Macadamia nuts have the hardest shell in the world, with three-hundred-pound psi needed to crack them. The kids and I would perch them one at a time on a lava rock and then, using another lava rock, hit them sharply to break and eat them. When raw, they were somewhat like coconut flesh. They didn't acquire their translucent crunch until after they were roasted.

One day, as I drove the truck around the orchard so Benjamin could load the full nut bags into the truck bed, the engine started to act funny. It was overheating. I had Jon and Misha with me in the front seat. It was a smaller truck, low to the ground, and the passenger door would not open from the inside. Suddenly, the engine gave a loud *bam*. I heard a scream from Misha, who was sitting next to me, but I saw no sign of Jon. He had vanished! The window had been rolled down about three-fourths of the way, and somehow, he'd shot through that small opening and ran as fast as he could away from the loud noise. Poor Jon was very frightened of loud noises; he would hide under the bed in his room whenever firecrackers exploded during Fourth of July celebrations.

We got good at harvesting and sorting nuts and scored high marks for quality from the local buyers, when we drove the nuts to market. High quality meant premium price.

You Can't Go

He would not allow me to leave the thirteen acres without a chaperone, and he kept the gate locked. A few times, I found him sneaking up behind me on my walks through the orchard and spying on me.

As August wore on, our oldest daughter, Aleena, called and asked if I would fly to her house to help out, due to the impending arrival of her first baby. We had sheltered her, and she was afraid to be alone without her original family. Her husband worked very long hours, so she was left alone most of the time, something she was not used to.

Before we moved from the mainland, Aleena had begged us not to leave, because she wanted family nearby when the time came for her baby to be born. Jason had promised both of us that he would allow me to fly back to be with her. He lied. When the time came, he would not allow me to go. Aleena begged and cried. She offered to pay all expenses for me to fly out and be with her but to no avail.

By the time she called in August, there was already a lot of tension between Jason and me. He did not like what I wore, everything I said seemed to irritate him, and he had begun calling me nasty names in front of the children.

"You idiot..." and "If you didn't have negative neurons, you would know... etc." "How can you be so stupid as not to see...?" and "Single digit IQ."

Among other expletives.

He would not allow me to leave the thirteen acres without a chaperone, and he kept the gate locked when he was gone. A few times, I found him sneaking up behind me on my walks through the orchard and spying on me. He made one of the boys go with me if I wanted to walk or bike outside of the gate. In retrospect, I think he was insecure about the new surroundings and wanted to make sure he had total control. I had been challenging him by getting my license, riding a bike, and wearing shorts or pants. No way was he going to allow me out of his control by allowing me to fly back to Washington by myself.

As a mother, I felt terrible. I wanted to do something to help my daughter, but I was too much of a coward.

"Please," Aleena begged. "Please let Mom come. I will pay for all expenses."

"No, she can't go. You can fly here and stay with us, but I will not allow my wife to leave," he told her on the phone.

He didn't say, "…allow your mom." He said, "…allow my wife." There's a big difference. He was letting her know that he owned me.

Of course, that was ridiculous. She had her doctor, insurance, and her husband there. She couldn't fly and stay with us, and he knew that.

The name-calling continued. It really bothered me that he would say nasty things to me in front of the children. In the past, he had made sure the children showed me respect; now he was showing them how to be disrespectful. He also said cruel things about our autistic son right in front of the child. During a trip to go snorkeling off of the west coast, Jason demanded irritably, "Why do we have to have Jon with us? We can never do anything or go anywhere because of him."

I was shocked that he would say that right in front of Jon, as if our son didn't understand what was being said about him. Jon understood completely—he rode in the back seat right behind his dad. Jon avoided Jason and didn't like to be around him, if possible. Earlier, I had encouraged Jason to take Jon out for a burger to help them bond. Jon liked that, but Jason complained that it just allowed Jon to be manipulative and get what he wanted.

The tension finally came to a head one day when Jason once again got mad at me and began to fling insults. He berated me, saying I had to live with him for another thirty years, so I had better do some changing. Then, furious, he slammed the door on his way out. I was dazed.

Another thirty years of this anguish?

It hit me like a sledgehammer: things were never going to get better.

I called my dad, and after explaining to him what had been going on, I asked him, "Dad, does God *really* expect me to put up with this treatment no matter how bad it gets?"

His answer helped to change my life. "Honey, God expects us to endure the normal ups and downs in marriage, but he does not expect us to put up with abuse." Then he told me, "Have your bags packed when he gets back and tell him you are not putting up with his treatment anymore."

Petrified and with adrenaline flooding my system, I began to throw things into our suitcases, packing our luggage with a certain amount of joy as well as overwhelming fear. Maybe I *could* escape.

When Jason got home and saw the packed bags, he became even more enraged. "What the hell is this?" he screamed.

Emboldened, I yelled back, and then we took it to the middle of the orchard so the kids couldn't hear us shouting or witness our fight.

We stood in the middle of the orchard screaming at each other, and for once, I finally told him the truth. I was done with his controlling me and treating me like shit. I told him I had not loved him since the morning, early in our marriage, when he told me to get up, even though I was sick, and make his breakfast, because he did not get married to have to make his own breakfast.

I told him there was absolutely no respect left after he had raped me, and then asserted, "You have only treated me like this because you believed I would never leave you, no matter what."

Being the perfect con man, he turned everything I said against me.

"I never would have done that if I knew *you* thought it was rape." That was not an apology. He then ripped me to pieces and spewed out anything nasty he could think of, threatening to ruin me and the children if I ever left him.

"I will sell the house, and you will have to live on the streets. I will destroy you financially and do whatever it takes to win. I *will* win," he spat out in fury.

By the time he finished intimidating me, I was crying with deep, gasping sobs. My fear would not allow me to realize that his threats held no real weight, because there was no way he could sell the house without my signature. I backed down. Trembling, I went inside and looked at the packed bags on the floor. I was crushed; desolation engulfed me. My two youngest wanted to know when we were leaving.

"We are not going anywhere," I answered bitterly. My heart sank to my feet, and self-loathing covered me like a shroud.

Jason was pleased with himself. He was victorious and in control again. His behavior afterwards confused me. He ridiculed me for not leaving, saying I was weak and had cold feet, and that I *"couldn't do it,"* in a sneering voice.

I had no idea what was going on with this man. He hated me, this I knew for sure, but why did he stop me, if he really did want me to leave?

* * *

My second grandson was born by the end of August without his grandma there. Aleena had a very hard labor and was damaged physically. She had no one to help her. Her own mother did not have courage enough to defy her narcissistic, sociopathic husband and come to her aid, regardless of his consent.

Jason may have won the skirmish, but I had changed that day. I no longer felt he had the God-given right to treat me like a kick dog. Life was not going to be easy for him.

When I called and told my father about my failure, he sympathized. "Well, maybe Jason got the hell scared out of him and will treat everyone better."

Unfortunately, my dad was wrong.

I could not bring myself to unpack the bags for two weeks. I left them in the living room in plain sight. The day I finally unpacked our luggage was an emotional one for me; I cried as I put away our clothes and things. I felt like a total failure. I berated myself and knew that I would never have the courage or the strength to leave him or assert myself.

If I could have seen into the future, I wouldn't have been so hard on myself.

* * *

By the end of August, we had to start schooling again. I insisted that we enroll the children in an outdoor Hawaiian school near Kapoho. I told Jason I was finished with homeschooling, which he didn't like, and yet, when we were done signing them up, somehow it had become his idea to enroll the children in the school. I left it at that. It may seem small, but every time I asserted myself, the tension continued to grow between us. In the past, I retreated and made Jason feel better by doing whatever I was told. Now, I sometimes stuck to my guns and dug in my heels.

Something my dad said about my treatment made me look up abuse on the Internet for the very first time. I always thought that "abuse" meant bruises and broken bones. I wasn't being abused… *was I?* I just had a bad marriage to deal with. After all, I had made vows, and you keep vows no matter how bad it gets, right?

Wrong. And I was shocked. As I researched the abuse cycle, I saw my own life revealed. Tears rolled down my face as I read about emotional, verbal, and psychological abuse. I easily identified Jason as a narcissist and sociopath; later, my therapists confirmed it—he *was* a sociopath and classic narcissist. They also said I was a classic victim.

The unrelenting anguish finally had a name…

Abuse.

* * *

So Benjamin and Jon attended school, and I often drove them out to the county road to catch the bus.

I also went to pick up Jon whenever he had meltdowns at school. Other than that, I was not allowed out of the thirteen-acre macadamia nut farm, unless I was chaperoned or had permission.

For several months, the school tried to accommodate Jon and his autism, but he was unmanageable. They had me come and monitor him. He would just get up and walk away from the school; he needed one-on-one attention. Sometimes he wandered into the road or behind cars that were backing up. He proved to be too much for the school to handle, so I returned to homeschooling him again.

Benjamin, now a young man, enjoyed the outdoor Hawaiian school. Besides the core curriculum, he was enrolled in a Hawaiian language class and a camp workshop for building ukuleles. The school was beautiful, with outdoor pavilions to shelter the students from the rain; new classrooms were being built across the road, on the other side of the property. The students learned many outdoor skills like woodworking, swimming, and lifeguard training at the Hot Pond next door. I thought very highly of the school.

Flesh-Eating Bacteria

> *I have never endured such acute pain—and remember: I went*
> *through labor ten times. The doctor stuck the instrument*
> *into the nasty-looking wound, and, as I gasped, he probed it.*

We often swam at the Ahalanui Park's hot pond. It is such a beautiful place, located right next to the school. However, there were posted warning signs that the water could potentially have bacteria; swimmers were instructed to shower after swimming and not to enter the water with cuts in the skin. I had a mosquito bite on the side of my leg and was told I would be okay, so I went swimming. The next day, the mosquito bite had something sticking out of it. Jason took a dirty needle and probed it. I mentioned that the needle was dirty, but he just laughed. When he probed the wound, it seemed numb. There wasn't much feeling. By the next day, it began to hurt. Quickly, the wound became badly infected, and my leg was in terrible pain from the foot all the way to my groin. Walking or putting any weight on it was agony.

Jason decided that the family would go on a day trip to west Hawaii. Only the two youngest children would accompany us, as

Benjamin was attending his camp for ukulele making. I told Jason that my leg hurt and felt I could not make the trip, but he insisted that it wasn't that bad, and we would mostly drive. He insisted strongly and would not take no for an answer, so we went to the King's Place of Refuge at Pu'uhonau o Honaunau National Park, on the west side of the Big Island. However, I could not walk on the recommended tour, and Jason was disappointed in me. We did have

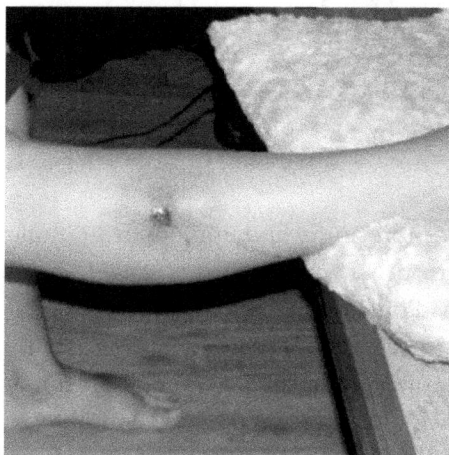

to get out and walk when we visited the beaches and were on foot around the stone walls at the Place of Refuge. I hobbled and that annoyed Jason. He was disgusted with me, and I felt terrible. I knew that he had little patience with other people's pain. By the end of the day, my leg felt like a lead weight, and the pain was excruciating.

The following day, I showed it to Dr. Mitch, the owner of the farms, who was spending some time working in the orchards. He told me he had been keeping an eye on it and was concerned about how fast the infection was moving. He decided to probe the wound, to see how deep it went. When Jason had probed it with the dirty needle, it was numb and I didn't feel anything, but it was painful even when my skirt brushed against it. I asked Jason to stay with me, because the probing would be done in the kitchen, and I wanted someone with me.

The doctor brought in his medical equipment, and I sat in a chair. Jason refused to stay and left, but then Benjamin came up and stood by my side, put a hand on my shoulder, and stayed with me. It was a bad thing for him to see. I have never endured such acute pain—and remember: I went through labor ten times. The doctor stuck the instrument into the nasty-looking wound, and, as I gasped, he probed it. He then cleaned and bandaged it. Dr. Mitch wrote a prescription for the second-strongest antibiotic available at the time. It cost $100 per tablet, and I needed five. Jason was upset and complained about the expense.

The doctor looked at him coolly and said, "It's either that, or she loses her leg and maybe her life, and if *that* antibiotic doesn't work, the only one left will cost $700."

Jason kept quiet after that, but I felt demeaned. I knew I was not worth it to him. How I wished he was the type of husband who felt I was worth it and was just happy to see me get well.

*   *   *

As time went by, Jason became more angry and upset with anything and everything. I tried to leave once by myself (just to see if I could) and go on a walk down the road outside of the gate; he quickly sent one of the boys after me to be a "chaperone." The gate was usually locked but not always, and I could get the key if I wanted to, but the unwritten rule was that I was not to go out of the gate without permission. Usually, Jason would leave with the key in his possession, and I once asked him, "What would I do if we had an emergency and had to get out?" It didn't seem to concern him.

Another time, I went walking around in the enclosed farm and found him sneaking after me, hiding in the trees and spying on me again. It was so bizarre. I have no idea what he thought I could do while I was locked in. Our son, Joseph, who had flown over early and cared for the farms until we could arrive, became concerned when he noticed how his father was treating me. Joseph began to take me on walks outside of the fence, and we also went for a few bike rides.

He would say things like, "Mom, you don't have to put up with this. There are other ways to live." And, "It is a choice, Mom. You can leave." A few times, he physically stood between me and his father when Jason became threatening and aggressive. Joseph, my gentle giant of a son, was by then much larger than Jason. He was a cycling enthusiast and was not only training for the Ironman but was bodybuilding, as well.

In December, the school was on break for three weeks, so we took advantage of that and reserved a camping spot in Spencer Park on the west side of Hawaii. Jason and I were cordial to each other but distant. We used Spencer Park as a base and visited the surrounding area. First we took Highway 270 up to Pololu Valley Lookout and hiked the trail down to the beach. The side of the trail was a sheer drop-off and incredibly gorgeous.

Jason stopped by one of the sheer cliffs and commented, "Wow, you could push someone off of here and no one would know it wasn't an accident."

It was a warning.

On the first night we camped, the nerve pain in my hips was so bad from lying on the ground that I couldn't sleep. So the next day, we drove into Waimaia, where Jason picked up sleeping pads for both of us, admitting he was too old to sleep on the ground, too. We then hiked the trails around Spencer Park, and the kids had fun surfing with their body boards at Hapuna Beach.

We really didn't plan well for the trip and only brought crackers, cheese, pretzels, peanut butter, and bread. I can only eat so many carbohydrates before I feel nauseous. Misha and I walked up to one of the stores near Spencer Park, and I spied a deli inside. There was a luscious-looking green salad with eggs and tofu. I struck up a conversation with the lady who took care of the deli, and we joked about how bad camp food can be. Then I ordered a large container of the green salad.

"How long have you been camping?" the nice counter lady asked me with a huge smile.

"Two days," I replied.

She gave me a funny look.

We went back to the farm in time for Christmas. A small potted palm was strung with lights and festooned with handmade paper ornaments for our Christmas tree. The other caretakers, Barry and Shayla, and our neighbor, Walter, came over for finger foods and drinks. The men sat outside amidst bananas hung up on posts, bulging bags of mac nuts, drying bins, tools, and hanging laundry, while Grandma Shayla passed out presents to the kids and then cuddled up with Misha on the couch inside.

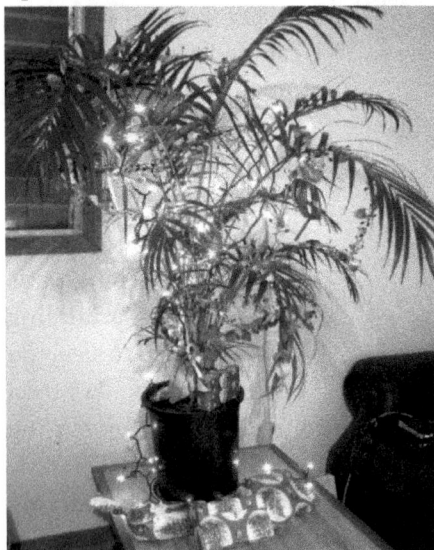

At the Catholic church in Lanoa, we attended a Christmas potluck get-together. The food was very good. A few months earlier, we had attended the veneration of the relics of St. Damian. A beautiful traditional hula dance took place outside the church to the sound of Hawaiian music, while a lineup of people streamed by to view the reliquary containing the saint's remains. The Lanoa church was one of the churches Father Damian had served at before going to help the lepers on Molokai, so the people in Lanoa had a great devotion to him.

Christmas in Hawaii was wondrous and yet fraught with fear. It was the calm before the storm.

CHAPTER 8:
STRANGE OCCURANCES

A man had died the year before, his body beaten to death on the rocks from the rough tide on the beach below… The very same area Jason wanted me to swim. A chill spread through me.

AFTER CHRISTMAS WEEK, WE WENT ON ANOTHER camping trip to the Kona coast. We went north through Hilo and then continued along the Hamakua coast through Waimaea and onto the Kohala coastline beaches. We stayed at Mahukona Beach Park the first night, a really nice park. It had an old sugar-loading dock area that was mostly decayed but great for swimming and snorkeling. Investigating a sunken ship meant even more fun.

There were two sides of Mahukona Park—one side had a loading dock area with concrete, a wall, and a ladder to get down into the ocean. That was the side with the sunken ship. The other side had minimalist campsites on rough ground along a rocky coast. The guys did some hiking around the area, and then Benjamin and Jason decided to go snorkeling to see the sunken ship. I wanted to check it out, as well. The ladder area of the dock was very slippery with a mossy algae-type growth near it. Misha and Jon were too afraid to

go down the ladder, and the water was choppy, so they stayed on
the concrete area and watched while I went in.

I swam around and found the sunken ship area. It was fascinating. Jason swam up to me while I attempted to see the ship
and suggested I dive down to see it. We were far from shore, and I
already felt tired and a bit out of my element, so I declined.

Then he encouraged me, "Swim over there." He gestured, point-
ing toward a distant rocky shore area on the other side of the docks.

"It looks pretty rough," I exclaimed, wondering why he wanted
me to go. An interior warning nudged my guts.

"No, it's great swimming over there," he countered. "Go on."

Instead of following
his suggestion, I swam
in the direction of the
dock area and got out.
I wrapped myself up
in my lime green batik
shawl, and Misha and
I took pictures of each
other. Then we went
for a walk and scouted
around.

We hiked over toward the area that Jason had pointed out to me, where he had indicated the swimming was great. On the top of the hill overhanging the rough rocky beach stood a cross and a warning to *stay away* from the area below and not swim there. A man had died there the year before, his body beaten to death on the rocks from the rough tide on the beach below. That was in the very same area Jason wanted me to swim... When he and Benjamin had hiked up the hill earlier, they had seen the warning. A chill spread through me.

* * *

Back home, when we had a chance, we spent some time snorkeling at the tide pools near Kapoho. There were many irregular pockets of marine life filled with exotically colored fish, various species of coral, a rainbow of anemones, and spidery-looking urchins. These natural pools were absolutely beautiful. I felt like a fish in a huge aquarium. No photo could ever do it justice. Navigating them could be tricky; the volcanic rock was sharp and rough but also slippery in places. The locals called these tidal pools the cold ponds, to differentiate between them and the hot pond at the Ahalanui Park.

The doctor's wife, Tanya, took me under her wing, and we went out to lunch together. I accompanied her to town when she drove the large truck filled with macadamia nuts to drop off at the buyers.

Over a delicious Thai lunch, she gently queried, "How would you like to live your life, if you got to choose?"

"Choose? What do you mean?" I felt a flush up my spine.

"Mitch and I've noticed how Jason treats you. So I have been wondering, if you had a choice, what would you want to do with your life?"

"I have no idea... I would like to be happy," I replied cautiously.

"Do you have any future hopes?" she continued. "Your life might not always be the same."

"I cannot imagine life being any different."

She went on to talk about other things, but her words echoed in my heart. Someone else had noticed.

First Joseph had talked to me about my life being different as had my father and now Tanya. Whenever I felt like I had to make a decision that was beyond my comfort zone, though, fear would take over. I had spent too many decades complying; persuading me to think differently was like trying to pry a barnacle loose from a rock. The efforts of others helped me to see that another life was possible. With their encouragement, I began to think that maybe I had a right to change my life.

If other people felt I had a right, maybe I did. Earlier in my life, I would have retreated, but the time was ripe. Jason was getting worse and life seemed more precarious and unpredictable.

*   *   *

Jason invited me to go fishing one day. That surprised me because, in the past, he always felt getting me a fishing license was a waste, since I got out so seldom. I had always wanted to go fishing before, but I did not trust him then, especially since my gut gave me that warning again, so I declined.

Afterwards, the thought occurred to me, *Maybe he is trying to be nice to me, and I should have gone.* Unfortunately, I spent a lot of time in denial.

Later that evening, when Jason came back late, he casually mentioned that he had taken Barry fishing with him. "I had to tie him to a tree," he said. "The drop-off was abrupt and steep—it sloped toward the cliff. There was no beach below, only sharp rocks, and it would have been easy for him to fall off the cliff to his death, so I tied him to a tree."

How bizarre! I thought. Out loud I replied, "Sounds like a dangerous place."

Much later, Barry revealed to me that he never wanted anything to do with Jason again after that trip, because Jason had spent the time badmouthing me and saying terrible things. That Jason would let me know a person could easily fall to their death, and that he had asked me to go along, was a blatant threat, a twisting of the screw, a warning that he was in control and that I'd better comply.

Toward the end of that week, Tanya took me to the cold ponds, just us two ladies, and we went snorkeling. It was great to feel like an adult, to get away and do adult things. That was, until we were packing up to leave after our swim, and Tanya asked me to go biking with her.

I automatically said, "Jason won't want me to do that."

She stopped what she was doing, looked directly at me, and said just one drawn out word, "Tessssy…"

The way she said it and the accusing look she darted in my direction made me flush with shame. I realized just how ridiculous my excuse sounded. In my inner hidden world with Jason, those were the rules. They were understood, and everyone had better follow the rules. When someone from the outside got a peek in, the rules were suddenly thrown into the bright light of reality, and they were ridiculous.

I had already gone snorkeling with her, so asking to go biking, too, would be pushing Jason's comfort zone, and I knew it. What she couldn't see was my fear. Jason and I were at a crossroads, and I didn't know where that would lead. In the summer, I had tried to leave him unsuccessfully and had been paying for it ever since. The innuendos of his being able to end my life were deliberate. He even bought a book on deadly marine creatures of Hawaii and left it on the seat in the car for me to see.

"Just so we know what to avoid," he said, when he noticed me looking through it. Nothing I could point at, no real evidence—just his way of interweaving threats into my life, subtly, relentlessly, until I bent back to his will or broke.

We continued our lives of macnut farming, hunting pigs, gathering avocados and other exotic fruit, and traveling whenever we got a chance. Except for the mind games and conflict, I loved living in Hawaii. I homeschooled the two little ones, and Benjamin biked to school.

The trip to school was all downhill—which wasn't too bad. But the trip back was all uphill, and he had a difficult time eating enough to fuel his bike trip every day. So he built a small engine onto one of the bike frames and began to motorbike to school instead. I was proud of his ingenuity.

Benjamin had a fine mind and was very gifted with his hands. He fashioned model ships, carved intricate boxes out of wood, and made his own ukulele. Unlike my husband, who never made me any gifts, Benjamin presented me with many handcrafted items, including a set of hand-carved mixing spoons. He was in the process of carving a fiddle and could play the banjo. His older brother, Joseph, could play almost any instrument he put his hands on. Some of the other children played musical instruments, too. Angela played the harp; Ryan, the electric guitar; and Alex played autoharp and the harmonica. Brent also plays the autoharp. All of the children were artists in one form or another.

It was January, and I chafed at being locked in the thirteen acres. The gate was open during the day, but whenever Jason left with the boys for any reason, he locked the gate. Regardless of whether there was a lock or not, there was a lock *for me*. I began to walk around the orchard in circles. I would take a stick and beat on the rocks and weeds with it to expend some of my frustration. Somehow, it made me feel better. The macnut trees were flowering in preparation for their main crop months later. The orchard smelled like honey, and bees swarmed around, buzzing happily. Old leaves crunched underfoot, and sometimes I found a lone macnut lying on the ground from the previous year, still encased in its green husk.

It was beautiful in the orchard. In some areas, the trees grew so close together that it was dark and cool, and when shafts of dazzling sunbeams shone through the trees, it was like an earthly cathedral. There were a few misfit plants and trees in the orchard, some of them "volunteers." For example, plump, delicious oranges hung from an orange tree; it had sprung up after someone spat out some seeds many years before. Papaya trees grew like weeds, producing lumpy papayas en masse around their trunk; they would then die within three years or so. A few of them scattered around the orchard, as well as six coffee trees planted by the former manager. There were banana trees and mountain apple trees, which were not really apples at all but a watery, bland-tasting fruit resembling a heart-shaped pear. There were also pineapple bushes topped with miniature pineapples scattered here and there. Benjamin made it his mission to cut off the top portion of each pineapple we bought at the farmer's market and plant it in the rocky lava ground. Soon they were putting down roots and growing into new plants.

One day, Jason came up to me and insisted I take a "ladies" day off.

"Take Misha, drive to Hilo, and spend the day shopping."

These suggestions of his had been getting weird. He did not even allow me to go out of the gate by myself. I had never once gone shopping by myself, taken any of my daughters out clothes shopping or gone to lunch for a "ladies day out." *What was going on here?* The tension had mounted relentlessly between us; this did not feel right to me. I didn't trust him; I had pulled back into my shell and refused to do any driving. Since Jon no longer went to the Hawaiian school, I didn't really have to drive anymore, anyway.

"No, I don't want to go to Hilo," I responded.

He looked confused. "Oh well—fine."

I felt relieved when he turned and walked away.

A few days later, Jason mentioned, after a trip to town, that he had almost wrecked the car. The tread on the tires had come apart and separated while he was on the highway, almost causing him to wreck. Immediately, I remembered when I had driven the car last; I'd mentioned to him that the car felt "wobbly" when it went over fifty miles per hour. It wasn't surprising that the tires had become shredded after driving over the rough volcanic roads. We had used the vehicle a lot and gotten it secondhand. It did leave me wondering just exactly why he wanted me to take it into Hilo, though...

Jason continued to be distant and unkind any chance he got. One time, several of us were sitting outside in the shade of the macnut staging area when he threw a derisive comment in my direction.

Benjamin, frustrated, explained, "Dad, *this* is how you treat a lady." Then he proceeded to pour me a glass of wine and talk in a gentle, kindly way to me.

It was to no avail—Jason wasn't interested. We sparred with words, and he became insulting. Joseph stood up, placed himself between us, and told his father to back down.

"You need to treat Mom nicer. I won't allow you to talk to her like that," he said, while trying to be conciliatory.

Jason's face hardened into a mask, and he looked away.

After that, Jason began to belittle Joseph, saying that he was lazy and we couldn't afford to feed him. Joseph was bigger than Jason and *was* a threat to his control, especially of me.

Jason decided to remove my protector. He told Joseph that he was no longer welcome to stay in Hawaii and needed to leave and go back to the mainland. Nice thanks, after the hard work Joseph had put in, in addition to flying over early and missing his sister's wedding so as to hold down the fort until we could arrive.

My big, gentle-hearted son did not want to leave me without protection. "I am afraid for your safety, Mom," he told me privately.

I was apprehensive, as well, but could not allow him to take the brunt of his father's anger, so I told him he should leave before things got any worse. A part of me no longer cared if Jason killed me. *How could my life get any worse?* I couldn't let myself think like that: my younger children still needed a mother... But the thought did occur to me, anyway. It was a coward's way of thinking.

During the last week of January, we drove to the west side of Hawaii two days before Joseph was scheduled to fly out of Kona and return back to the mainland. We camped at Spencer Park and drove Highway 270 north along the Kohola coast to do some sightseeing. We stopped off at Mahukona Park again, but I did not go swimming that time. While Jason and Benjamin swam, they found an eight-foot manta ray in the water, and Joseph spent his time relaxing and tanning.

On our way back south, we stopped off and toured the Hamakua Macadamia Nut Company. I was glad we stopped because, in my opinion, it was the best nut-candy shop on the Big Island. They sold T-shirts that said, *Got Nuts?* I had to laugh at that. We had toured the better known Mauna Loa plant the year before. It was a larger operation with lots more to see and delicious nuts and candy, but I preferred the chocolate confections produced at the Hamakua Macadamia Nut Co.

On that Tuesday, we took Joseph to the airport, and I hugged him tightly goodbye. My protector was leaving, and I did not want to see him go. Little did I know I would be following in his footsteps a little over a month later. I guess, in retrospect, I should have realized that, with Joseph gone, the situation would deteriorate.

* * *

We had been planning a spring trip to the mainland to see our new grandchildren and visit my parents in California. The mac nuts wouldn't be coming in again until the summer, so it was a good time to go. Aleena had a new baby, and Angela's firstborn was on the way. I would have the chance to see my oldest grandson—Alex's son—and visit with some of our older children.

When we got back from our trip dropping Joseph off at the airport, I made reservations for four of us (Jason, me, Jon, and Misha) to fly out of Hilo in April. Since we were planning to be gone for about six weeks and Benjamin was still in school, he wasn't included in the trip plans. He would stay and manage the farm under the watchful eye of Barry and Shayla. He would be sixteen by then, and even though he didn't drive until later, he didn't need to because he had access to the free public transit system that circled the Big Island and was strong enough to walk the few miles to catch the bus to town for groceries and essentials. He had matured quickly in the last year and was quite responsible. I was very proud of him.

Now that Joseph could no longer protect me, Jason redoubled his efforts to be cruel in small, backhanded ways. However, Benjamin noticed, and he stepped between us a few times. Increasingly, I felt tormented and filled with anguish. I didn't know it then, but my mind and soul were going through a fight—the fight for my life. I was too scared to make a move; I was paralyzed with fear. And yet Jason had come up with several life-threatening situations.

When we went to the hot pond, Jason would pester me and get mad if I didn't show him affection publicly at the pool. Then he would follow me around just to annoy me. I took to floating on my back and looking up at the palm trees, imagining with razor clarity that I was free and he was no longer in my life, no longer controlling me. I didn't realize it then, but I was *manifesting my future*. I didn't know what manifesting was, but I was zoning in on being free, feeling free and... being alive.

The gate was locked more often after Joseph left. I took to walking the orchard in circles again, angry and chafing at being penned in like a criminal, which, to Jason, I was. During the trip to the westside beaches on an earlier weekend, I had worn a large, loose tank top over my bathing suit and shorts. Although I had worn the same attire many times to go swimming, for some reason, on that weekend, it enraged him that I had dared to wear a tank top. It wasn't a tight tank top; just a man's loose tank top. As the tension continued to increase between us, eating became difficult for me. My stomach was often in knots, and I was losing weight.

Jason had every reason to be upset; I was no longer the same doormat he was used to controlling and was asserting myself. Emotionally, I had withdrawn; my senses were on high awareness as I tried to figure out what he planned to do next and thwart any dangerous moves he made. It felt like I lived in a combat zone. And all along was also the pretense that nothing was wrong—we were a holy little family, going to church every weekend but remaining outside. (Jason wouldn't go inside the church; he preferred to stay outside on benches that were set up for overflow crowds.) We even fought over allowing the children to attend catechism classes, which he later claimed were his idea, once I ended the fight by simply signing them up. Any time he lost a power struggle, he redoubled his efforts to squash me back down under his control.

The pressure mounted as he began to demand more. Any chance he got, he displayed his anger and cruelty. The mind games were constant and woven into every aspect of our lives, I was no match for him. At night, I would wait until he fell asleep and then carefully, silently, let tears stream down my face. Once day, when he left the farm and locked the gate, I went out into the orchard and prayed as I paced in circles around the rows of macnut trees.

I had reached a breaking point.

"Why won't you open my prison (let me die), God?" I asked Him to take one of us, because I was still so narrow-minded and felt that leaving was impossible. "Take me," I cried.

But then I thought of the children left alone with Jason for the rest of their childhood, how he taunted and pestered Jon without remorse, and how Misha was afraid to be alone with him. "No, take him. *Just end it!*" I begged. Often I had wished Jason would die; now I was asking for it. "You alone have the key, God. Open my prison!" I begged, as tears streamed down my face. I convulsed with sobs and sat down next to a tree.

And then—a still small voice inside me seemed to say, "*You have the key in your own hand, and always have.*"

It was the turning point. At that moment, my decision was made. For three decades, I had been determined to honor my vows no matter how bad it got, but now I was just as determined to escape and be free of him, no matter how difficult it was.

It was a decision Jason had carefully ensured that I would never be able to make. He had let me know for years that there was *no way out* of our marriage; he had made sure it was theologically tight. There would be no divorce in our marriage. He was absolutely certain of it. The Church would never allow an annulment, and so he would own me forever.

I called my dad, and together we decided that, when we took our trip to visit them in April, I would refuse to go back with Jason and would instead stay at my parents' with the kids. My dad was concerned that Jason would become violent, so he called Joseph and got him to agree to be there at the same time, for our protection. None of us knew what we were doing. Joseph called me and was supportive and relieved that I had finally decided to leave.

Immediately, the terrible anguish that had been tearing me apart left. It was replaced by another stress: the stress of knowing we would be escaping but not for several more months. I would have to be careful not to betray myself to Jason. He would know that something was up. It would be hard to contain myself as my situation worsened and every day seemed like forever.

February crawled by. We got some goats for weed control, and they ran around the orchard pooping everywhere and eating everything, especially the cat food, if they could get to it. The weight continued to fall off of me, my heart beat erratically, and my insides were shaky. I was a nervous wreck. The knot in my stomach would barely allow me to eat more than a few bites.

Jason noticed, but I laughed it off, saying, "I must have picked up the bug Benjamin has."

Benjamin was also having a difficulty eating; his stomach hurt and he had indigestion. I thought he must be stressed out, too, with his parents fighting all of the time and the terrible tension in the household, but later found out he was sensitive to coconut. It irritated his intestines and gave him diarrhea... We were eating a lot of coconuts in Hawaii.

*   *   *

After being given some purple sweet potatoes, I made two purple pies and some purple muffins with white crumb topping. They were pretty and gave me something to post about on my sourdough blog. At this same time, my sourdough book had been reviewed by three different publishers; a famous baker friend gave my spirits a boost by listing my sourdough site as a resource in his newly published book. He sent me a signed copy, and when I read my name in the resource section, I gasped in surprise.

My two youngest were happy to do their homeschooling and then play in the orchard. Gentle Misha named the goats, and they went running after her as she played.

Jon didn't like the goats; he was afraid of their unpredictable behavior. Since the mosquitos loved him, he would run around in the warm weather with a long-sleeve shirt, long pants, a floppy hat, and an umbrella that he loved to carry around. With his goofy grin and lovely, innocent face, he was adorable.

Oh God, why, why did I not see? Why did I allow them to suffer so much? My sweet babies, my loves, you are the reason for me still being alive.

If you have never lived with a narcissist, you would have no idea how they contort reality into a dark labyrinth of pain and anguish, how they pretend to love you or care about you only to turn on you to destroy you. Your thoughts and words are warped until you have no mind or thoughts left. You are always wrong, and they are always right. You doubt your own sanity and don't know how to act or what to do next; you never know what's coming or what innocent thing will be used against you to destroy you. They must be in control, must win, can never be unmasked; their wonderful veneer to non-victims must be intact. If you dare to do or say anything to disrupt their carefully crafted fantasy world, you will be turned on with hatred and vengeance.

I was alone with this monster. I shielded the children the best I was able to from his twisted workings. They did not always escape. He knew I loved them, and he used them to keep me in my place and control me. Who would ever believe the convoluted maze of mind games? Would there be anyone in my corner, when no one really knew what was going on? I felt so alone.

In the end, he got careless. Different people witnessed his usually hidden behavior. He got careless because he had us isolated and thought I would never leave him, no matter what. He had brainwashed me for decades to obey him, to do what he wanted, and made me believe that I could never leave, that it would offend God and I would go to hell.

It was too late. I was already in hell.

The days went by agonizingly slow. I no longer cried silent tears in the night but was hollow inside, filled with a black endless hole. I tried to put my mind on hold. The fear was so great in me that I couldn't think of what might happen when we faced him off at my dad's.

How did I continue on? How did each day turn into the next day?

> *Hawaii, the sun, the waves, it is warm. I am on my back floating, and I see above the coconut trees. The clouds. I will be free. I will escape. Spencer Park, he rages at me. He hates me. He has hated me for a long, long time. I do not know how to be hated. My heart is hidden. Scared. Safe. Hide. Do not go home. Do not ever see him again. Run away. He hates me. No do not touch me. Oh my god, I hate him. do not touch me. Go away. Die. Die die die die. Pretend. Hold it together. No one knows. Hold it together, you can do it. Walking on the road. Joseph will keep me safe. Run away. Leave. Gated in. imprisoned. Hated. Pretend. You can do it. Only 9 more years. You can do it. I cannot do it. I cannot do it. Hit the tree, hit the rock, hate. God help me get out. God help me. God go d god godgod… the keys god, I need to get out of here. Help me! Tessy. Get away. Detach. Anger. Rage.*

*Hate. Unpack the bags. Cry. You cannot do it. You cannot
do it. More hatred. You will sleep in the marriage bed. I
hate you you whore , you terrible terrible awful., hate anger,
rage please god help me escape, my god love me. If someone
would just love. Me. Why? Why? Someone somewhere god,
is this all? Why? It is cold. I need him to have a warm heart.
Love me. I am so broken. There are too many pieces. Will
you gather up the pieces? Will you love them all? You do
not understand, I cannot tell you what it was like.*

— Tessy's writings

Escape!

*He towered over me, raging like a volcano erupting, spewing
the ash of hate, raining down words to destroy me, raping
my soul, tearing my insides to pieces. A wave of molten
hatred washed over me. I shrank down into the couch.*

We went to the west side of Hawaii to meet up with Jason's sister and
her husband, who had flown in from the mainland for a Hawaiian
vacation. We met them for a few hours at Spencer Park and enjoyed
swimming together. Jason expressed horror that his brother-in-law
dared to wear a man's bathing Speedo in front of me. That weekend, it was very windy on the westside. A tsunami had just struck
Hawaii, and the ocean was still quite rough. After Jason's sister and
her husband left to explore the island, we went back to camp, and I
asked Benjamin if he wanted to go for a walk.

Immediately, Jason's face hardened.

Benjamin noticed and quickly said, "Why don't you ask Dad to go?"

I looked at Jason with his blanched face and narrowed eyes and
asked him, "Do you want to go for a walk?"

He spat out, "No, you don't want me to go. Just go with Benjamin."

I did not feel like playing the game, so I turned to Benjamin.
"Let's just go."

EPILOGUE II

JASON INTERFERED WITH THE ANNULMENT PROCESS by trying to influence the Catholic Tribunal of Monterey, CA against me. (The case was transferred to Seattle.) He then tried to gamble our shared marital possessions on the outcome of the Tribunal's decision, offering to give me everything if the decision went in my favor, which he was certain would not happen.

In December 2014, the Seattle Catholic Tribunal finally granted the annulment in my favor (no, Jason did not give me anything).

All is forgiven. I've moved on with my life and I hope Jason has found happiness.

Darkness.
I reject darkness; it will not be my natural state.
It will not win.
JOY. I CHOOSE JOY.
No one will ever again force me to live in darkness.
—TL Reys

ABOUT THE AUTHOR

Tessy Reys Gannon is a pseudonym. The names of people and most—but not all—of the places have been changed to protect the individuals involved; however, everything that is written in this story is true and actually happened, according to the author's point of view.

Tessy now lives with her two remaining teenagers, Jon and Misha. Jason still lives in Hawaii. The rest of the children are raising their own families, and Tessy has ten grandchildren and counting.

Feel the Wonder!
On golden wings spread
joy meets the sunrise
wild elation freedom brings
soaring higher

Crushed, broken, bruised, discarded
foaming water, waves racing on the shore
feet burrowing in the sand
oh sweet joy! Heart contracts

Arms opened wide
encompassing all pain, joy, ugliness, rage, love forgiven,
forgotten, past, swept away in the maelstrom
come hear the silence, feel the wonder

I am free

—Tessy L Reys

If you know a silent victim who might benefit from reading this memoir, please share it with them.

Photos for this memoir can be found online at:

http://www.reach4joy.com